Welcome...

...to the Back to Basics issue in which we'll look at all the major tools, features and filters of the new version of Paint Shop Pro 9

Includes lessons and step-by-step tutorials explaining the new features

THE OFFICIAL PAINT SHOP PRO® LIBRARY

#06 Back to Basics
A complete guide to the features, filters and tools in the all-new version of Paint Shop Pro

INCLUDES 10 PRACTICAL LESSONS AND 22 VIDEO TUTORIALS ON THE CD

A 132-page full-colour guide to both the basic and advanced new features of PSP 9, including the host of new filters guaranteed to improve your digital photos

Jasc Software

PC CD-ROM
450Mb+ OF PSP 9 VIDEO TUTORIALS

THE OFFICIAL PAINT SHOP PRO LIBRARY
TOOLKIT

PAINT SHOP PRO 9 TRIAL
Try out the latest version of PSP for up to 60 days.

FILTER FRENZY
No fewer than 10 full, unrestricted, plug-in filters for you to incorporate into your copy of PSP

600 Free brushes to paint with

PLUS Original images for you to follow tutorials with

Jasc Software
Demo pack of brushes from Brush Foundation

Paint Shop Pro has had a major update and to celebrate the fact that your favourite image-editing package has just got better, we're going right back to the beginning to examine how everything works. While this will be familiar territory for old hands, the Library has had a change of publisher this issue, so insights into how the tools work and what should work better are given from a different perspective. And that perspective comes from myself, the new editor of The Official Paint Shop Pro Library. Here's just a little of my background for you – as well as having been a technology journalist for some 18 years, I am also a professional digital photographer and the author of digital photography books.

Anyway, according to Jasc's own market research, there are two types of PSP user – those who want to create images, either as artwork for a variety of purposes or for webpages, and those who want to improve their digital photographs. That's why the improvements to this release of PSP are split between the purely photographic, in terms of digital camera tools and filters, and the artistic, with the provision of the new Art Media layer, paints and brushes.

In this issue we're going to look at how everything works, what has been improved, what the new features are and how you can use them. At the end of every chapter we've provided the usual Lessons. These include step-by-step tutorials, either to using the interface and tools or to making improvements to your photos.

On the Toolkit CD there's a trial version of Paint Shop Pro 9, so if you use version 8 you can decide whether you think it's worth upgrading. We certainly do. There are also 10 new plug-in filters for you to use in PSP, which provide a variety of fantastic effects. Add to this some 600 new brushes, and you're well on your way to making the most of your investment in the software. Whatever your skill level and expertise, we hope you'll enjoy this issue and join us again for the next one.

Duncan Evans
www.duncanevans.co.uk
Contact: editor@psplibrary.com

OUR AIMS

In each book, we aim to provide the highest-quality Paint Shop Pro advice available. We want to teach you something new each time so that you build your expertise as the series progresses. We also promise to deliver the very best dedicated Paint Shop Pro resource CD possible. We will fill each disc with video tutorials, extras for Paint Shop Pro and add-on filters, brushes and software. Our aim is to make this series worth every penny. If we miss something you wanted covering, let us know at **editor@psplibrary.com**.

DON'T MISS OUT

This is an ongoing series of books so to ensure that you don't miss out on any of them, why not subscribe to the series? You can save money and ensure that you get every copy. Turn to page 126 or go to **www.psplibrary.com** to find out more.

Live Publishing International Ltd

Europa House, Adlington Park, Macclesfield, Cheshire SK10 4NP

www.livepublishing.co.uk

EDITORIAL

Editor	Duncan Evans
Sub Editor	Rachel White
CD-ROM Interface	Fizzy Media

techsupport@livepublishing.co.uk

01625 855051 (Monday-Friday 10am-4pm)

PRODUCTION AND ADMINISTRATION

Design	Tym Leckey
Production Controller	Debbie Whitham
Financial Controller	Karen Battrick
Editorial Director	Wayne Williams
Group Publishing Director	Robin Wilkinson
Circulation Manager, UK	David Wren
Circulation Manager, International	Steve Hobbs

Distributed through the newstrade by Comag
ISSN 1743-2278
Printed in the EU
All contents © Live Publishing International Ltd

SOFTWARE USED IN THIS GUIDE

We have used Paint Shop Pro 9 on a Windows XP computer to create this guide. If you are using a previous version of Paint Shop Pro you may find that some of the features are missing or work in a slightly different manner. You can still try the features using the Trial version of Paint Shop Pro 9 included on the CD. We recommend that you upgrade to the latest version so that you can experience all of the power it has to offer.

SUBSCRIBE TO THE SERIES TODAY!

Subscribe online at
www.psplibrary.com
Subscription and back issue enquiries to
01625 855140
This series is dedicated to helping you get the best out of your images with Paint Shop Pro. The series will show you how to use every feature it offers through a combination of tutorials, video walkthroughs, creative lessons and more. Each issue comes with a specially created Toolkit CD-ROM.

The Official Paint Shop Pro Library
Back to Basics

Contents

Contents

Each chapter and lesson detailed, plus a full listing of the video tutorials to help you get the most from this guide

12 Chapter One Paint Shop Pro's user interface

We look at what's changed in the user interface, how the dialogs and tool palettes work and the completely new features of Paint Shop Pro 9. Three of the features detailed here include the Mixer and History palettes and the Print Layout function.

32 Chapter Two Back to image basics

We cover image resolution, a fundamental aspect of image creation and print production. Being able to cut, copy and paste images or parts of them as new images, layers or objects enables you to construct entirely new projects – find out more here.

44

Chapter Three All about brushes

Brushes are the tools by which you apply effects, so it pays to know what the options are, how to create new ones, and what the standard brush tools do. The Clone tool is incredibly useful – we'll cover this here and a host of others

60

Chapter Four Photographic tools

This new edition of Paint Shop Pro has been produced with the requirements of digital photographers in mind, hence the addition of the Digital Camera Noise Removal and Chromatic Aberration Removal tools, plus the Fill Flash and Backlighting filters. Turn to page 60 for more.

82

Chapter Five All about layers

While they may seem difficult to understand, layers are actually very powerful tools and are capable of everything from image composition to sophisticated photo editing. The new feature we'll look at here is the Art Media layer.

92

Chapter Six Using text to better effect

You can have text as a selection, as a bitmapped image or as a vector. With the latter option, resizing is easy and the words can be assigned to a path you create, no matter how curved or twisted it is. We'll show you how...

Contents

98

Chapter Seven Using special effects
Paint Shop Pro 9 has a host of filters. Some have been organised into new Art Media categories and others have been spruced up. All your old favourites are also included. Some, like the Displacement Maps and the lighting effects, are very powerful indeed, as you'll see.

104

Chapter Eight Images for the Web
Aside from editing digital photos, the other main application of Paint Shop Pro is in creating graphics for webpages. Here we look at some of the options for image preparation, like creating buttons and utilities such as JPEG optimisation.

110

Chapter Nine Borders, frames and edges
Using edges and frames can really set your images off, but you need to know what can or can't be done with them, what is built into Paint Shop Pro and how you can create your own edge effects. Find out here...

116

Chapter Ten Device integration
Adding new hardware is easier than ever before, but getting devices to surrender their images without a fight is the key to this chapter. You'll learn about accessing digital cameras and using the new Raw filter option.

122

Chapter Eleven The Official Paint Shop Pro Library Toolkit
This is the guide to the contents of the Toolkit CD. It also provides a helpful page of key terms, information on how to subscribe, what's in the next issue, and a handy index.

MISSED OUT ON ISSUES 1, 2 or 5?
ORDER BACK ISSUES TODAY– turn to page 130

Video Tutorials

As we're going back to basics to celebrate the launch of Paint Shop Pro 9, the video tutorials show beginners how to get to grips with the program, and also introduce many of the new features

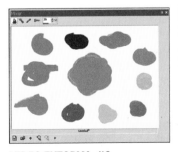

VIDEO TUTORIAL #3

Mix and spread paint with the Mixer palette

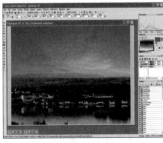

VIDEO TUTORIAL #9

Learn how to put together a layered image

VIDEO TUTORIAL #19

Get funky with text that follows strange paths

Book conventions

This is an example of a standard dialog. You will see this type of user interface in all Windows programs

This is how menus and sub-menus work. We would reference this as View/ Palettes/ Layers

This is just one of the palettes available in Paint Shop Pro – there are many others

The Tools toolbar, shown floating, contains icons that provide access to the image-editing tools. Paint Shop Pro offers many other toolbars

Throughout this series of guides we will use the same conventions to make it easy for you to understand. We have aimed to make everything as friendly as possible, but if you are confused by what we mean, this page should give you the answers to both our conventions and simple terminology. You will find a glossary of the more technical terms on page 125.

Dialog – We refer to all dialog boxes as dialogs. This is the computer terminology spelling and it means any box that opens within the program when you click on an icon or a menu option. Dialogs can look very different. In Paint Shop Pro, some of them are standard Windows dialogs (like the Open file dialog) and some are idiosyncratic to the program, like the Effects dialogs.

Menu items – We have used a standard convention for references to a menu item or a sub-menu (a sub-menu is an item in a program menu that has additional entries that appear when you put the pointer over it). The convention is menu name (which appears at the top of the program)/ sub-menu name (if applicable)/ menu item name.

CD-ROM files – The CD that accompanies this book is integral to it. It not only includes all the video tutorials that you will find

numbered on many pages, but also tutorial files for the walk-throughs, additional information files and extra material for Paint Shop Pro. Whenever we reference a file, we give you the folder path as folder name/ sub-folder name/ filename. Go to the CD and navigate through the hierarchy in this way to open the file. The video tutorials are all executable files that can be found on the CD. The CD also has an interface that facilitates its use.

Toolbars – There are several toolbars in Paint Shop Pro and we use their default names. A toolbar is the part of the interface that contains icons that you can click on to perform an action. Some toolbar icons are part of a group and include a drop-down menu signified by an arrow you can click on. We reference these as we do the normal menus. The name of the toolbar will be shown as part of the toolbar if it is floating, but not if it is docked (attached to the sides of the program interface).

Palettes – Palettes look very much like toolbars, but don't offer tools themselves. Instead they provide options for the tools in the toolbars or additional editing features. The Materials palette is what most people think of as the traditional artist's palette (it's here you select colours), but it is only one of many in Paint Shop Pro.

Part One
Paint Shop Pro

CHAPTER 1

Paint Shop Pro's user interface

The user interface makes the program's functions readily available for use with your images. It can be customised to suit your desktop resolution and working practices

The Paint Shop Pro user interface hasn't changed since the previous release, so if you are upgrading from version 8 there is very little to be afraid of. If you are a newcomer to the program though, the plethora of icons, toolbars and palettes can be confusing. In this opening chapter we'll guide you through installing the program, then we'll look at the main toolbars and their functions. This kicks off with accessing picture files, browsing and sorting, before we move on to look at loading and manipulating.

There are toolbars and there are palettes. Toolbars generally contain options for manipulating and accessing files and specific functions.

They are initially docked underneath the drop-down menus, but can be grabbed by a handle on the left-hand side of the bar and dragged into the working space, or docked on any of the sides of the working space. When a toolbar is already present on one side, another toolbar to be docked there will be added to it if there is the space to fit all the icons on. The toolbars can also be hidden from view.

Palettes are similar to toolbars but are usually found on the right-hand side of the interface. They usually contain information about an image that has been opened, or if nothing is open, then either a list of tools that can be used or nothing at all. Palettes can also

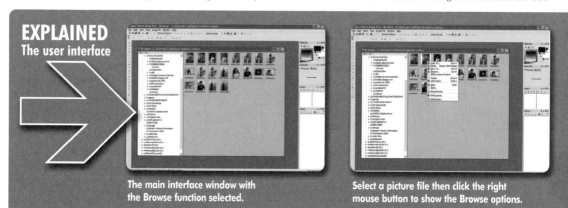

EXPLAINED
The user interface

The main interface window with the Browse function selected.

Select a picture file then click the right mouse button to show the Browse options.

be turned off, moved around as floating items, or docked on any of the sides of the interface.

The main toolbars and palettes

Standard toolbar – Concerns file management and provides access to the Browse feature. It usually sits underneath the File drop-down menu and there is little need to move it from there.

Browse toolbar – This enables you to sort, select and search for images, then load them for use in the program.

Tools toolbar – The heart of PSP, this contains the tool set you will use to manipulate and edit images. It is normally docked on the left-hand side of the screen.

Effects toolbar – This provides access to the Effects browser and contains a limited selection of the main effects.

Photo toolbar – A one-stop guide to quick fixes for photos, including everything from barrel distortion to dodgy colours.

Tool Options palette – Here you can specify exactly how each tool will be used, when you are using it.

Histogram palette – Very useful for assessing the overall tonal balance of a picture, or examining the RGB and H/S/L components in-depth.

Layers palette – An important palette in image composition that enables you to use Adjustment layers to selectively improve an image.

MORE TOOLBARS AND PALETTES
There are also toolbars for Script, Status and Web functions, and palettes for Brush Variance, Materials, the Learning Centre, Overview and Script Output.

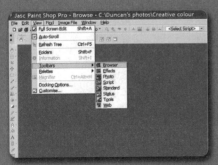

The View menu controls the visibility of the toolbars and palettes.

Toolbars can be picked up and moved around the interface, or docked again.

VIDEO TUTORIAL #1

The first video tutorial shows the Browse function being used to examine options and load an image. For serious photo-editing work we recommended you use a monitor capable of supporting 1,280x1,024 resolution or higher.

Installing PSP 9

While installation is straightforward, there are some choices to be made along the way

UPGRADING?
If you are upgrading from a previous version of Paint Shop Pro you should uninstall that version before proceeding with the installation of this version. If you do it the other way round you run the risk of removing vital shared files from the new version.

When the Paint Shop Pro 9 CD is inserted it will automatically launch the installation wizard. This has a default installation location and it lets you choose which components you put on the hard drive and which you leave on the CD. If you have enough hard drive space, it will save you much needless searching for the CD at inconvenient times if you simply install everything. Where you install it is up to you, but the usual Program Files folder is as good a place as any. Once installation is complete the program's icon will appear on the Start menu – you can also place a shortcut icon on the desktop. You will be given the opportunity to register the product online. This isn't an annoying Microsoft-esque 'register or else' process but simply an option to register and receive updates, PSP freebies and information.

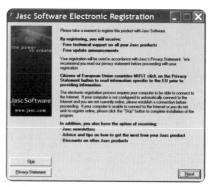

Register the program online and receive a number of free downloads

SPLASH SCREEN
Version number information can be found on the splash screen

The splash screen appears when you run the program and, usefully, shows what version is installed. Periodic updates are made to PSP by Jasc and once installed, the new version number will register here. If you are unsure at any point which version number you are up to, go to Help and About Paint Shop Pro and and you will be presented with this screen.

A time-limited trial of version 9 can be found on this issue's CD

STEP BY STEP

INSTALLING THE PROGRAM

1 Insert the CD and the autorun menu will appear offering a choice of the products on the disc. Select the option to install the program. If the program has already been installed, the Program Maintenance menu will appear (inset). This allows you to change the installed features, repair PSP if vital files have inadvertently been deleted, or uninstall the program entirely.

2 This is the main option screen. From here you can determine which features are installed on the hard drive; aren't installed at all; and can be called upon by inserting the CD.

3 After installation you are given the option of having the program check for updates. Note that you will need to be connected to the Internet for these checks to be carried out. You can set the frequency from daily to never.

4 The final step is to assign file associations to PSP. There are a lot of file types listed here, many of which you'll never encounter. Unlike some programs that assign every file invented to that program, PSP is quite conservative, meaning the default associations are acceptable if PSP is going to be your main image-editing program.

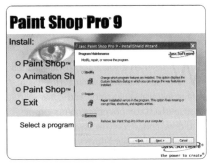

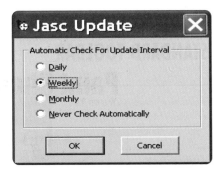

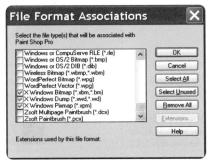

FILE ASSOCIATIONS
Associating file types with PSP means that when you double-click on any file type that is linked to the image editor, the program will load first then the file will follow.

Standard toolbar

This toolbar offers Open, Save, Print and other fundamental functions

BITS OF INFORMATION
When creating a new image, the bit depth specifies how many colours it has. Use 24-bit (16.67 million colours) for regular photographic images, 8-bit (256 colours) for Web graphics and 4-bit (16 colours) for Web banners.

In version 9 of Paint Shop Pro, the Standard toolbar and Browse function have changed slightly and have become simpler. The standard features of Open and Save are exactly the same, and if you are a regular computer user you'll find these will behave as you would expect. Obviously, the Browse button launches the Browse function, which is used to navigate through thumbnails of picture files, making it easier to select one. Users of Windows Me and XP will be familiar with the concept of thumbnail browsing, though here there are extra features available. Also on the Standard toolbar is the TWAIN Acquire button, which is largely redundant on modern systems that use Windows XP. On older systems this was the standard method of connecting to a scanner and some of the very earliest digital cameras.

The Standard toolbar doesn't normally float around the screen with the word Standard displayed. It's usually docked just underneath the File drop-down menu. If you click and hold the left-hand side of it, it can be dragged and dropped into the working space, then dragged back again.

Clicking on Open reveals a standard interface, in which the files can be displayed as thumbnails

IN DETAIL **THE STANDARD TOOLBAR**
The very basics of PSP

1 The New button creates a new image, with a user-definable colour or transparent background. The image resolution and print density can be set along with colour bit depth and a choice of three types of background – Raster for pictures, Vector for line-based artwork and Art Media for artistic endeavours. See page 24 for more details.

2 The Open button opens the standard Windows file browser, which can be set to show thumbnails. In the bottom right-hand corner of this is the Browse button. Click on this to launch the PSP 9 Browse function.

3 The Browse function can be started directly by clicking on this button. The Browse toolbar itself is

hidden by default and isn't actually needed anymore, as you'll discover on the opposite page.

4 The Save button allows files to be saved in a variety of formats with different degrees of compression where available.

5 The Print button starts the Print dialog, which controls the printer driver itself. See page 28 for more.

Browse toolbar

Searching for images can be a painstaking business — the Browse function makes it easier

The Browse window opens when you click on the Browse icon on the Standard toolbar. A new addition to version 9 is the left pane containing the Find and Info functions that can be applied to files. The Browse toolbar itself is hidden by default, but should you wish to, you can display it by selecting View/ Browse. However, nothing on the bar will work until the Browse window itself is open. The initial Browse window shows drives and folders on the left and picture files as thumbnails on the right. It also only shows half of the features. If a picture file is selected the other functions become available. These functions can also be accessed by right-clicking in the folder contents area or on a file. This is a faster method of working and cuts down on unnecessary toolbars and icons, which is why the Browse toolbar is initially hidden.

The functions are split into two groups as mentioned. The first set deals with copying, renaming, moving, opening and deleting images. The second provides find, refresh, sizing, browsing, selection by criteria, sorting, updating and panning options. Other features can only be accessed by right-clicking on files. These include a lossless rotation procedure for JPEG files, information details, an option to send the image, photo sharing and print layout facilities.

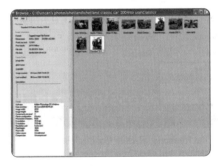

WINDOWS XP USERS
Most of the Browse window's functions can be found in general folder use in Windows XP, including the ability to rotate JPEG files to their correct orientation. It's the sorting and selection tools of the Browse window that set it apart, as well as the fact that it operates within the PSP interface, meaning files can be found more easily without going outside into the general Windows environment.

The Browse window showing picture thumbnails and the new Info panel

---

IN DETAIL THE BROWSE TOOLBAR
Find your way around the Browse toolbar to search, select, copy and move with ease

1 When clicked on, the Copy (1a) and Move (1b) file options both show a pop-up box that is used to navigate to the destination folder that the file will be copied or moved to.

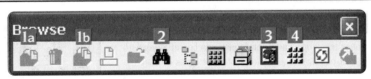

2 The Find button allows you to search for text that is part of a filename. Unfortunately, this only works for the folders that are linked to the one you have open, either upwards towards the root directory or downwards into sub-folders. You cannot select the root directory of the hard drive and search every sub-folder downwards, which would be its most commonly required and beneficial use.

3 Select is also a search option. It allows you to select files based on criteria such as filename, size and date, and image attributes, like width, height, bit depth and size.

4 By using the Sort option you can categorise images by name, extension, date, file size and type, or a set of image attributes. You can then sort them again into secondary categorise using the same criteria, with the exception of name.

Tools toolbar

This is the most important toolbar in Paint Shop Pro so you'll need a good reason to hide it

TOOLS FOR TOOLS
Tools can be used in various ways – access these via the downward arrows next to the icon or on the Options palette.

The Tools toolbar is usually docked on the left of the screen with its title hidden from view. There's no mistaking the contents though, as this is the heart of image editing in Paint Shop Pro. In version 9, the toolbar can be undocked and resized into different shapes to fit the working area. This is an improvement on version 8, in which it could only be viewed horizontally or vertically.

Amongst other things, the tools available allow you to move the image around and zoom in and out. There are also selection, deform and photo-enhancement tools. Icons with a downward arrow contain different types of that tool. For example, Zoom and Pan are on the same icon space because they are directly related to each other – once you've zoomed into the image, you'll want to pan around it without having to use the scroll bars on the image window. Usually, once a tool is selected the Tool Options palette shows the variations that can be used with it and how it will work.

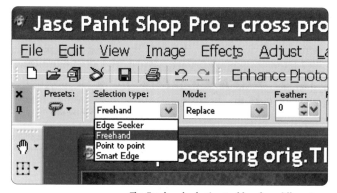

The Freehand selection tool has four different settings that affect how the process works

IN DETAIL THE TOOLS TOOLBAR
Whether drawing of deforming, the tools you need are accessed here

1 The Deform tools include Perspective Correction, Straighten and Mesh Warp. These are useful for correcting simple barrel distortion problems, converging verticals, or more creative use.

2 The Selection tools include object-shaped or freehand selections. The Freehand Selection tool has four variations. The type of image you're working with will determine the selection tool necessary. For example, the rectangular selection tool is no use for cutting around someone's hair but it's perfect for cropping a photo.

3 The Clone and Scratch Remover. This is an invaluable tool that's used for restoring old images, removing things from new ones, and cleaning them.

4 The Emboss tool is a bizarre choice to head this group, which otherwise consists of extremely useful tools for spot adjustments of pictures.

5 You'll either never use the Picture Tube or use it all the time. Its value lies in the quality of full-colour clipart you use with it, as it is essentially a spray can for such images.

6 The Chalk tool is the head of the Artist Materials tool set. Everything from drawing to oils is represented.

Tool Options

Select a tool then determine how it's used with the Tool Options palette

The Tool Options palette is a set of variables applicable to the tool that is currently selected. As each tool is selected, a different set of options appears in the palette. Some of the tools work in similar ways, even though the results are very different, so these will have the same or very similar options – Paintbrush, for example, offers a set of options that is duplicated across many other tools. Others, like the Freehand Selection tool, are used for a totally different purpose, so the options they provide are radically different. It's important that you understand which of the

options associated with each tool is critical to using it properly. The Clone tool's Opacity option, for example, has a radical effect on how this tool can be used – the wrong setting spells disaster. Fortunately, if you have upgraded from Paint Shop Pro 8, you'll find that the options are just the same, though resizing brushes has been made easier.

EFFECTS OF OPTIONS

The usefulness of the options varies – some only have a slight effect while others have a critical effect. As you use the tools, explore the important features of their options.

The Paintbrush offers a standard set of options that is duplicated across many of the other tools.

The Freehand Selection tool, on the other hand, is completely different.

IN DETAIL COMMON TOOL OPTIONS
These options are found across the range of tools

1 There's a variety of shapes available that can be used for brushes. For ordinary purposes there is little point in using anything other than a circular brush, but you may occasionally need to use specific shapes. Painting (Art Media) is just one area in which brush size matters.

2 There are a number of ways of changing the brush size, including the new method in which the line under the brush shows how big it is. Grab this and a sliding scale of dots shows you the increase in size. Drag it to use it.

3 This sets the density of the edge of the brush. Hardness set at 100% means it does not have a feathered edge, so its use will be sharp and apparent.

4 This determines how close together the pixels in the brush are. When using Art Media this can have a very important bearing on the result.

5 The Opacity is extremely important for a number of tools. While it represents how visible the effect is (expressed as a percentage), what it actually determines is the strength of the effect you are applying. For the Clone tool and image-retouching tools, this is a critical variable.

Layer palette

At the heart of image composition and photo editing lies an understanding of layers

LAYERS IN ACTION
To find out more about layers, turn to Chapter 5. Then, when you're feeling confident, why not have a go at the Lesson at the end of that Chapter?

Whether you are simply editing photos to make them look better or creating a multi-part compositional extravaganza, knowing how layers work is vital. Layers in Paint Shop Pro 9 are much the same as in version 8, with the exception that a couple of the blending modes have changed in terms of how they work. For compatibility, the old modes are also still available. A layer can be a photo (a bitmapped raster image or a vector image) shapes or text, or it can now be Art Media materials. Blending modes determine how layers interact, while opacity determines their transparency. These two key factors allow disparate elements to be blended together. Turn to Chapter 5 for an in-depth look at layers.

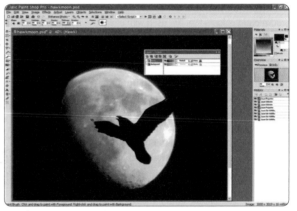

There are two layers in this simple composition. The hawk has been cut out and is on a transparent background, while the moon forms the main background

IN DETAIL **THE LAYER PALETTE**
Sat on the right-hand side of the screen is the Layer palette, which is essential to image composition

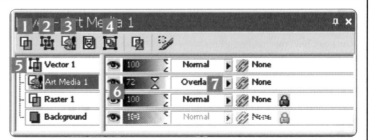

1 This icon creates a new Raster layer.

2 This one creates a new Vector layer.

3 This is for Art Media layers. The Art Media layer is different in that it can use canvas effects.

4 Group layers together using this icon, making them easier to edit during large compositions.

5 This shows the name of the layer. The layer being edited is highlighted, even if it is not visible.

6 The eye icon indicates that the layer is visible and the value to the right shows the percentage of visibility.

7 The blending mode specifies how each layer will combine with the one below it.

Materials palette

The one-stop shop for colours and textures for your images

When you want to paint, touch up or create new images, the Materials palette is the place to go. It's also the palette to visit to set the foreground and background colours that are used with everything from painting tools to text and flood fills. The Materials palette sits on the right-hand side of the screen and has a coloured box surrounding a palette of shades of one specific colour. To change the shade click in different areas of the colour box. Above this box are three tabs that show the existing colour frame box, a rainbow selection of colours, and a selection of colour and material swatches.

To the right of the colour box are the foreground and background colours, which have smaller icons underneath. The first of these is multi-functional, allowing you to swap between the use of a solid colour, gradients or patterns. Next to this is an icon that shows whether a texture is being used, and at the end is one showing whether transparency is involved. There is a difference between the application of patterns and textures. Textures are used on the surface and combine with the painted colour; patterns are the colour of the paint, but are specific, repeating shapes.

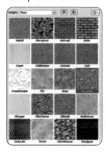

TEXTURES
There are three types of texture with plenty of variety in each one. You can also create your own textures.

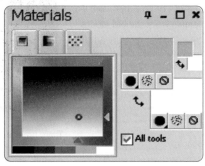

The Materials palette not only provides access to colours but textures, patterns and gradients as well

---

MATERIAL PROPERTIES
Select gradients and patterns, and create your own colour swatches via Material Properties

Double-click on the foreground or background colour to bring up the Material Properties box. This has entries for colours, gradients and patterns in the main section, and textures on the right. The colour selector is easy to use, combining a colour wheel and shade with RGB and H/S/L components below. You can set the colour by entering individual values into these. H/S/L stands for Hue, Saturation and Lightness, which essentially means colour type value, the amount of it and the underlying monochrome tonality. Unless you have a specific reason not to, sticking to

Red, Green and Blue (or RGB) is the safest bet.

The Materials palette also contains swatches, which are splashes of colour. As they stand they aren't much use, it's when you create your own that their potential is realised. If you are using a specific colour in a number of images, say for a typeface, set it up here and click Add To Swatches. Your custom colour will then be available in the swatches list. Gradients and patterns can both be manipulated (which includes rotation). A standard gradient will run from light to dark, but you can change the way the pattern runs.

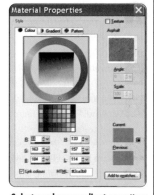

Select a colour, gradient or pattern from the wheel. Next add a texture to the painted effect

History palette

Everyone makes mistakes, but luckily this feature allows you to go back in time and correct them

VIDEO TUTORIAL #2

Discover how to delete actions out of sequence and create Quick Scripts that you can save for later use

An efficient undo system is extremely handy, especially in image composition; you'll want to try out things, then be able to return to the critical point step by step if they don't look right. With version 9, Paint Shop Pro has acquired a new undo system in the form of the History palette. This records each and every action you take on an image. Each action can then be undone in sequence. Many of the processes can be undone independently – when this isn't possible the

action is marked as undoable. The system will also mark a set action as undoable after a certain number of steps – this feature is customisable.

The only drawback of a sophisticated History palette system is that it takes up a lot of hard drive space. By going to File/ Preferences/ General Program Preferences then clicking on the Undo tab you can see the preferences for this. If you don't have lots of hard drive space you might want to click on the Limit Undo tick box and set the storage required per image to something like 200MB. The alternative is to limit the amount of undo/redo steps. By default this is set to 250 steps, which will cover even the most ambitious project. The more steps the program records, the more space it takes up, so something like 50 steps is perfectly acceptable for modest image-editing projects.

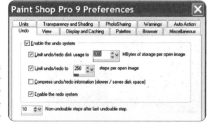

Setting the preferences in which the History palette works will limit the hard drive space it will occupy

IN DETAIL THE HISTORY PALETTE

The History palette can save you lots of wasted time if a project goes horribly wrong

1 This option will undo everything from the last action to the currently highlighted one.

2 This undoes a single action. It can be the most recent or any other that you select if it is possible to undo it out of sequence.

3 This is a very useful option that allows you to create QuickScripts from actions listed in the History palette. Mark a number of actions then click on this icon to save the sequence as a QuickScript.

4 This switches the status of items that have been undone into ones that cannot be undone. You'll find it useful when you undo something that you then realise is a critical action.

5 Empty the entire History palette here. This is useful when you are running short on space as it clears all the Undo saves.

6 This item is an action that has been selectively undone.

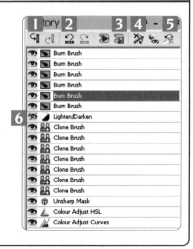

Mixer palette

If you're feeling artistic, don't limit yourself to everyday colours — create your own

This new feature of Paint Shop Pro 9 allows you to mix your own colours to create combinations that you can paint with. Obviously, the most useful application of this is with both Art Media materials and layers. The Mixer palette is hidden to start with, so go to View/ Palettes/ Mixer or press Shift+F6 to bring it up on screen. Like all palettes it can be docked or left to float freely. The problem with docking it is that you need lots of space for colour sampling and mixing, and the window really isn't big enough for this if you have it docked. The mixing area extends beyond that initially shown on screen and if you are feeling particularly adventurous, you can customise its size. The downside to this is that you have to click on the Navigate icon to pan around the rest of the workspace. You'll also have to select the Mixer Tube to return to squirting colours onto the palette or the Mixer Knife to scrape them together. If you are intent on using natural media materials, a far better practice is to undock the Mixer palette and make it wider, giving you room to experiment.

The Mixer palette offers step-by-step undo and clean-the-slate options. You can also save palettes for later projects.

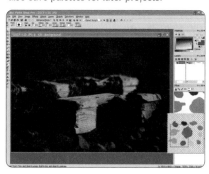

VIDEO TUTORIAL #3

 The mixer palette can be used to mix different colour paints to form new textured paint that can be used with the Art Media brushes

When docked the palette is too small to be used for mixing more than a couple of sample colours

---

IN DETAIL MIXER PALETTE

Get creative with colours by creating new ones

1 This is the Mixer Tube, which squirts the colour onto the mixer page.

2 The Mixer Knife drags paint in the direction that you scrape.

3 The Mixer Dropper is used to select a colour out of the mixer for use.

4 Red and yellow colours have been mixed together here to create an orange tone.

Remember that the Mixer palette can only be used with single colours which it then gives subtle variation to. You cannot use patterns, textures or gradients here.

5 The Unmix button steps you back through individual stirs of the paints.

6 This icon reveals the Mixer Palette menu, which allows you to save, load or wipe clean palettes.

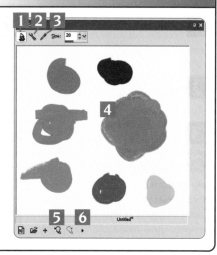

New images

All new projects begin with the creation of a blank canvas

DENSITY & SIZE
The image density and dimensions set when you create a new image have implications when you come to print it out. For more on this turn to page 28.

If you often build new compositions, design graphics for your website or copy and paste sections of images, knowing how to create a new image is a necessity.

You can create a new image by: clicking on the New Image icon (which looks like a blank sheet of paper) that's found on the Standard toolbar; selecting New from the File menu; or using the Control+N shortcut. Once that's

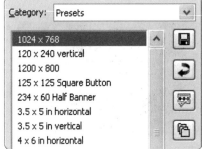

PSP 9 offers a range of commonly used preset sizes, suitable for Web graphics, small-print size pictures, and more

done, a dialog box appears that asks you to choose from the preset sizes or gives you the option of creating an image of your own size by setting the width and height.

An initial choice of Background layer types is provided, from Raster (for photos), Vector (text and objects) and Art Media (painting). You will also need to select the colour depth. This largely depends on what you are using the new image for, but 24-bit uses 16.7 million colours and is the standard for photographs.

You may occasionally want to create a new image after copying something to the Clipboard using Control+C. In Photoshop it is necessary to create an empty image before you can paste in the new data. In PSP, however, you can paste directly from the Clipboard to create a new image. By pressing Control+V you can produce a new image with the dimensions of the original.

IN DETAIL NEW IMAGES

There's more than one way to import your images into PSP

1 This is the Preset drop-down list, which contains a wide variety of image sizes for print and the Web.

2 The image dimensions are set here in pixels, centimetres or millimetres.

3 The resolution is set here. This is a general setting that has no real meaning when editing on screen because by zooming into an image you will change its pixel per inch (ppi). What it does is set the print density, so when you go to print, a scale value of 100% will use the resolution density for printing and set the print dimensions.

4 This is the initial choice of background types available.

5 The colour depth affects how many colours there are in an image. The standard colour depth is 24 bits. Using fewer colours for Web banners will save on file size.

6 The Transparent tick box sets whether the image has a colour as its background or is empty.

7 The dimensions are repeated again here, but for good reason as they also show how big the file will be.

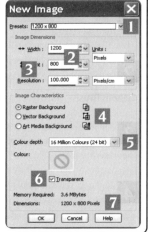

Opening an image

The starting point of your activities in Paint Shop Pro

There are a number of ways of opening an image in Paint Shop Pro, the first of which is the Open (file) icon on the Standard toolbar. This brings up the standard Windows dialog box for file navigation and image loading. The icon on the right that has a downward-pointing arrow enables you to view files within the window in different ways – as thumbnails, for example. If you are looking for a specific file type, like a JPEG or TIFF, click on Files Of Type and select the file type required.

When a picture file is clicked on, image size and colour depth information appears at the bottom of the dialog box along with a small preview picture. By clicking on the Browse button in the bottom right corner you can launch the Browse function.

Another way of using the same Open function is by accessing it via the File menu. Pictures can also be easily loaded by simply dragging them from a Windows folder and dropping them directly into the interface.

NEW FOLDERS
PSP's Open function uses a standard Windows dialog, so you can create folders by clicking on the relevant icon just as within Microsoft's program

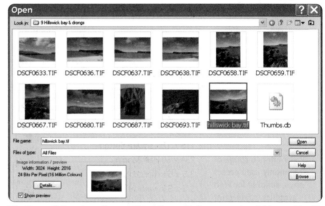

The Open dialog shows image dimensions – find out more by clicking on Details

---

IMPORTING IMAGES
There's more than one way to import your images into PSP

Importing is the function by which images are loaded into PSP from an external source, rather than from the hard drive. The option is found under the File menu and allows you to import custom brushes as well as images from external sources. The options found under Import are as follows.

Custom Brush – You don't just have to use the brushes supplied by PSP: you can use third-party designs or brushes you've made yourself in the correct format.

Screen Capture – This menu entry has two further options: one to configure the process and the other to actually do it. It allows you to set up PSP to capture the screen, usually from other applications, and then imports the image directly into PSP.

TWAIN – This is the old-fashioned method by which digital cameras used to connect to computers. Virtually everything these days will offer either a serial option at worst, or a USB or FireWire connection at best, to connect directly to the computer. Surprisingly though, many cameras are still shipped with a TWAIN driver, even though this isn't the best way to connect to the computer.

From Scanner Or Camera – This might seem to be the same as the above option, and indeed it is. The difference, however, is that it uses a method of connectivity known as the WIA connection protocol. To use this option your Windows system needs to be XP or Me and the scanner or camera must also use the WIA connection system. When connecting your device by USB, the contents can be directly imported into PSP without having to go through a File browser first.

Saving an image

Don't degrade an image's quality – ensure you save it in the right format

FILE EXTENSIONS

The three-letter extension after the full stop in the file-name describes the file's format to Windows. Always use the correct extension for the file type. If in doubt, type in the filename and leave the extension blank – all modern software packages will add the correct extension for the file type being saved.

If you've created a new image from scratch or you've imported one from the Clipboard, you can use the Save option to give it a file-name and select the file type. This option is accessed by clicking on the disk icon or select-ing Save from the File menu. Whichever you do, the Save As dialog box will appear as this is a new image. Thereafter, when you resave the image it will simply save it with the current file-name and file type. When working on an image it's worth preserving the original and giving the new working version a different name. To do this, select Save As from the File Menu and change the filename and file type.

The initial Save As menu lists the files as names, but Me/XP users can opt to view them as thumbnails. You can navigate around folders or create your own to put the file in, but perhaps the most important button in this dialog is labelled Options. Paint Shop Pro can be quite

sneaky here as this might include options that you don't want, so be sure to check it before saving. For example, when saving as a TIFF file it will automatically include LZW compression to make the file smaller. That's fine, except that some programs can't read LZW compression because it's a licensed technology that they don't want to pay for. The exact options you're given are dependent upon the characteristics of the file type.

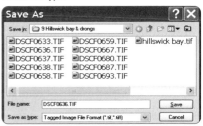

In the Save As dialog, remember to click on Options to set your own preferences

SAVE AS OPTIONS

Choose the right options to ensure your target audience can view the image

As previously mentioned, the exact options available are dependent on the image type being saved. Some use specific compression systems and others reduce colours. The JPEG file format is the most commonly used for digital pictures, so let's have a look at the options for this.

Encoding – There are three choices here, with the default one being Standard, which offers access to all the Save As features. The Lossless Encoding option saves the JPEG without any loss of information or quality, but still compresses it, thereby saving space. Progressive is a slightly more aggressive file saving option, and is a matter of bytes as it doesn't save any EXIF information. EXIF is picture and file metadata that

is embedded in any image. Digital cameras utilise it to record the parameters used to take a photo.
Compression Factor – This directly affects the quality of the JPEG image. The more compression you use, the smaller the file size and the poorer the quality.
Chroma Subsampling – This is the degree to which the compression routine will analyse and compress the data. The further down the list you go, the more compressed the picture will be, but the poorer quality will become.
Run Optimiser – You are also given the option to run the optimiser, which provides a preview of the quality of the version you will be saving. This is very handy if you have to heavily compress a file but need to check it retains a certain level of quality.

Common file types

Understanding the differences between the file types is essential for their everyday use

OTHER FILE TYPES
PSP supports about as large a selection of file types as it is possible to imagine, even going back to the days of the Amiga. If you want to load graphics created for older systems, you'll probably find them supported here.

1 PSP Image (.pspimage or .psp) This is Paint Shop Pro's proprietary format. It will save all the layers, objects, Raster, Vector and Art Media information. It can be saved uncompressed or using lossless compression. It can also be saved to be compatible with previous versions of PSP, but doing so will result in the loss of more recent features. Only those with a copy of the PSP version you save the image to be compatible with will be able to load it.

2 Tagged Image File Format (.tif or .tiff) This is the standard format for high-quality images. It supports layers, which leads to larger files, and can use lossless compression to reduce the file size. However, some applications (shareware in particular) don't support LZW compression, so if you need to compress an image it is recommended that you use the JPEG format. If you need it at the highest quality, use an uncompressed TIFF.

FILE SIZES
The four file types seen here were the following sizes:

PSP – 17.4MB

TIFF – 17.4MB

JPEG – 906KB
(20% compression)

GIF – 904KB
(256 colours)

3 Joint Image Experts Group (.jpg or .jpeg) Most digital cameras use JPEGs by default because they take up less space than other formats. You can save JPEG files at 100% quality, meaning they won't lose any information, but as soon as the compression is increased the quality is reduced. Every time a JPEG is resaved it re-samples the data and compresses it again, so subsequent saves reduce the image quality further. Only save a file as a compressed JPEG when you've finished working on it.

4 Graphic Interchange File (.gif) This is a Web-based file format that was pioneered by CompuServe. The advantage of GIFs are as follows: they can use a very limited colour palette, which drastically reduces file sizes; they can be interlaced so that as the file appears as it loads; and they can use transparency. The disadvantage of saving an image as a GIF is that the format it limited to 256 colours, which isn't very good for photos.

Printing an image

Controlling how your images are sent to the printer is key to successful output

PRINTER OPTIONS

While Windows XP has a marvellous hardware database, its printer options are somewhat lacking. You will need to install a printer driver that comes with the printer in order for it to be usable by all Windows applications, including PSP.

Select File/ Print to bring up the Print dialog box. First specify whether the image should be portrait (vertical) or landscape (horizontal) in orientation.

The Size and Position settings are in millimetres – take careful note if you're used to working in inches. If you know the paper size you are printing

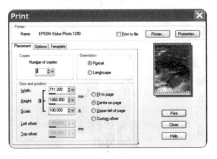

Use this dialog to change the size and orientation of your image

to in millimetres, set the width and height and PSP will scale the image to fit. You can then specify where on the page the image should be anchored. PSP doesn't resize the image dimensions, merely the printing density, which it portrays as a scale percentage. A spot of maths and a calculator are required to work out the actual dpi you will be printing at, and what the resulting quality of print will be like. Instead, we recommend leaving the Print menu for a moment and using Image/ Resize to resize your picture before printing.

The simplest way of getting the image to fill the page is to tick the Fit To Page. However, if you do this you can't specify where on the page the image can be anchored without recourse to the Print Layout option.

PRINTER PROPERTIES

This is where you'll find the real nuts and bolts for controlling the printer

Use this dialog to specify whether colour or black ink is used, how much ink is used, and the paper type the ink will be printed on

From the Print dialog box, click on the Properties button (or click the Printer button followed by the Properties button), and the printer's own driver properties box appears. This dialog is entirely model and make dependent, as manufacturers offer different styles of presentation and levels of control.

You can usually set colour or black printing here. This is not a decision you should take lightly for black and white images, because the colour option uses all the ink tanks and produces a high-resolution print. But be aware that a colour cast may result. If you opt to use black, your printout will be coarser as only one tank will be used instead of four, six or eight.

The paper type you select affects how much ink is sprayed on the paper. Choose the incorrect type and you could end up with soggy prints or prints with banding and weak colours. Photo-enhancement options are usually available and it's down to you to decide whether to use these, as the colour management system of PSP isn't its strong point. That said, it can be worth trying to see what the results are like. Setting this type of option to custom or manual usually means you can control individual ink tanks and how much each one uses. The strength of black ink can usually be set as well, so if prints are too dark or oversaturated this can be resolved.

STEP BY STEP

USING PRINT LAYOUT

1 The Print Layout option is used to place a single picture on a page or, more usefully, a number of pictures on a page. These can be anything from holiday snapshots to photos of a model for her portfolio, as is the case here. Load all the pictures you want to use into PSP, then select File/ Print Layout.

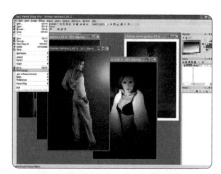

VIDEO TUTORIAL #4

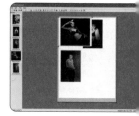

In the video tutorial we show you how to load, organise and caption pictures using Print Layout.

2 The loaded images will appear in a strip down the left-hand side of the screen. Drag and drop them into the layout area. A prompt will be activated that asks whether you want to scale the pictures. Say that you do and use the handles in the corners of the images to resize them. The aspect ratio is preserved, which makes this easy. Click on the pictures and drag them to wherever you want them.

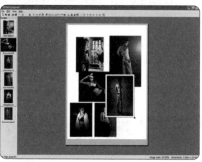

3 There are a couple of options that help you arrange your pictures. If the pictures are straight from a camera, they can be rotated so that they are the correct orientation. More usefully, the AutoArrange button will intelligently rescale and arrange your pictures into rows and columns, based on their shape and size. Images can be rescaled to exact sizes and there is a host of simple arrangement options to hand.

4 The Open Template icon provides access to a wide variety of template layouts for numerous combinations of same-size or disparate images. New for PSP 9 is the captioning feature. By clicking on the Text icon you can place a caption anywhere on the layout. The font, size and colour can all be set but be aware that they apply globally to everything within that text field. To use a different size font, create a new text field.

LESSON 1
Batch processing

Save yourself time and effort by processing lots of files, all in one go

Digital photography encourages you to shoot like there's no tomorrow. You aren't paying for film, so the tendency is to photograph everything in range. That's great, but sorting through the files later can be very tedious, which is where batch processing comes in. There are three real applications for batch processing: for renaming files so that they have proper names rather than a string of numbers; for turning photos to the correct orientation; and for resizing and saving as JPEGs for Web use.

The Batch Process function in Paint Shop Pro runs script actions on the images selected. The actions do all kinds of things, including adding artistic effects, mono conversion, splitting channels, sharpening and adding borders. The only trouble with these is that they're a lazy road to mediocrity – the process will be exactly the same for each image, regardless of the content, colour or shape. A professional certainly wouldn't see this as a good way of treating high-quality photographs. If you're simply shooting lots of family or holiday photos then a process that carries out a modest amount of work on colour, contrast and sharpness is perfectly acceptable. You'll have to create this yourself, but fortunately, the Scripting wizard makes this easy.

Scripts vs batch processes

The Batch Process uses scripts, whether they're already created for you or you create them yourself. If you don't use any script options then all the Batch Process can do is rename and save the file in a different format. Batch Rename is a useful and much simpler way of doing this.

Scripts sound scary, but at their simplest they are very easy to record and use. A script is a set of commands that PSP processes and carries out. PSP supports a full scripting language called Python, but to edit scripts using this language manually really requires a proper script editor, as the syntax and spacing of the commands are critical. For standard photo-editing tasks this isn't necessary.

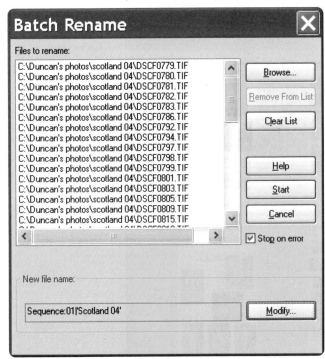

Add number sequences and a new generic name using the Batch Rename tool

STEP BY STEP

RECORDING A SCRIPT

1 Load the first picture to carry out the processing on it that you want to turn into a scripted action. Go to File/ Script/ Start Recording. This activates the script recorder, which logs all the processes you carry out. For the purposes of this lesson, go to Adjust/ Brightness/ Curves. Enter an S shape curve to increase the tonal range of the image.

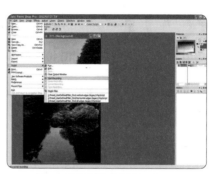

2 Now go to Adjust/ Hue and Saturation/ Hue/Saturation/Lightness. Increase the saturation by 20% – this is generally the most you can comfortably increase the saturation by without making the image look gaudy. Digital noise effects may also begin to appear should you increase the saturation by anymore.

3 Now go to Adjust/ Sharpness/ Unsharp Mask and enter 2.00 for Radius, 40 for Strength and 4 for Clipping. This gives a modest sharpening boost without causing too many problems with haloes where object borders differ, on plain surfaces, or, notably, on the horizon. Click on Save, then go to File/ Script/ Save Recording. Make the file-name something descriptive so it's obvious what it does.

4 Go to File/ Batch/ Process. Use the Browse button to select all the files you want the process to run on. Tick Use Script then select your custom script from the list. You might want to put the new pictures in a sub-folder called Corrected Pics until you're confident about using the process. In that case, click on New Type and set the correct file type and location. Otherwise, click Obey Script which has the Save option in it. Finally, click Start to run the process with your script.

VIDEO TUTORIAL #5

The video tutorial shows how to create a script and then use it in a batch-processing task.

EXTRA OPTIONS

Putting a tick in the Stop On Error box means that the program will stop if there is a problem during the batch process. If the Silent Mode is ticked it will stop and won't do anything else. If the Silent Mode box is left unticked, the program will ask you for a decision regarding the problem. If there isn't problem and the Silent mode isn't ticked, the program may ask about over-writing files or similar tasks.

CHAPTER 2

Back to image basics

Almost everything you do in PSP will call upon these few basic lessons in image creation and manipulation. Here we explain some basic procedures that will get you started

This chapter looks at the basics of image and print sizing, selection tools and basic cutting, copying and pasting. There's virtually no difference here between versions 8 and 9 of Paint Shop Pro, so if you are an old hand at this you might want to jump to Lesson 2 (page 42) before moving on to the next chapter.

Assigning information to an image is one way either you, the creator, can ensure vital details are fully credited, or a digital camera can record the settings used when a photo was taken. When recording personal information you don't need to fill in reams of details, just a basic copyright warning and any pertinent comments to ensure that your intellectual rights to the pic-

ture are duly noted. The information stored by a digital camera can be very useful, particularly as it's often almost impossible to remember which settings you were using at the time. This is stored in the EXIF data part of the file.

Image information can be accessed via Image/ Image Information, or by pressing Shift+I. The initial menu tab shows the location, dimensions and storage size of the image. The printing dimensions are also given and these are directly related to the pixels per inch (ppi) setting shown. This is easy enough to change – see the step-by-step guide to the Resize option on page 35.

The Has Been Modified entry in the Status

EXPLAINED
The Image Information dialog box

The Image Information tab covers everything from the image dimensions and print size, to the location, status and file size.

Add your details, copyright notices and description of the image here, but remember, only certain file types (and not TIFFs or JPEGs) save this.

section refers to a modification that's been made by PSP specifically. It also shows whether there is a selection saved with the picture, and if it is a multi-layered file. As for the number of colours, a photograph will invariably have a 24-bit colour depth offering 16.67 million colours. If it's a digital photo that was saved in-camera in monochrome mode, it will only be 8-bit, offering 256 shades of grey.

The Creator Information tab allows you to enter names, copyright notices and comments to identify and describe the image. The Watermark Information tab provides access to a tool you have to pay for, that enables you to mark your picture with an identifying code to prevent copyright theft.

The last tab is EXIF Information, and for digital cameras this is where the good stuff is stored. It provides the following information: camera and manufacturer, original date of creation, resolution, exposure mode, screen program, exposure compensation, shutter speed and aperture, Automatic White Balance setting, ISO rating and focal length. The tick box enables you to display everything or just items with data values. Unless you have the camera connected to a GPS receiver, these values are likely to be blank.

To record copyright or author notes in the image information, ensure you save the image in a PSP-native file format, or as a Photoshop PSD.

EXIF DATA

You can only edit a few items in the EXIF data as its purpose is to record information from the camera. So unfortunately, there's no way of changing the exposure values from point and shoot characteristics in order to make yourself look like a hotshot.

The watermarking service is provided by the Digimarc Corporation and has to be paid for. Watermarks help prevent copyright theft.

The EXIF Information is a goldmine of image details from digital cameras. You can learn most things about how an image was taken here.

VIDEO TUTORIAL #6

Follow the video tutorial to learn how to enter your copyright information into the image, or check how it was taken if it's a digital camera picture.

Image resolution

The number of pixels in an image directly affects the size at which it can be used

DIGITAL CAMERAS

Particular terminology is used to refer to the image resolution of pictures that digicams produce. They're are referred to in terms of millions of pixels, or, megapixels, written as Mp. The number of megapixels is arrived at by multiplying the pixel dimensions of the image and rounding it off – for example, a 2,400x1,600 resolution image is a 3.8Mp picture.

Digital images are made up of pixels – one pixel is one coloured dot. The more there are, the more detailed the picture, the bigger it can be printed or used, and the more room the resulting file takes up on your hard drive. Image size is another term for image resolution, but file size is the amount of space required to store the picture.

Image resolution affects what you can do with a picture. If it has a low resolution and you print it out at A4, the lack of pixels will be apparent, causing the image to have jagged edges. You can resize an image to do two things: increase the actual amount of pixels (a process called interpolation) and set the dpi, or print density of the image. The dpi refers to the amount of pixels in each inch of the printed

picture. This figure must be quoted in conjunction with the image resolution to be useful; if, for instance, a picture is referred to as 4Mp in size, you'd know how big it is, but simply referring to it as 300dpi is meaningless as it could be any size.

The amount of pixels in an image determines the level of detail. For landscapes, 6Mp is the bare minimum

RESOLUTION EXPLAINED
Get to grips with common terms

Pixels Per Inch (ppi) – This is the number of pixels that are present in every inch and is often referred to as a screen resolution. It isn't really worth worrying about because as soon as you zoom into an image, the ppi changes. The ppi is used to ensure that when the image is displayed on other people's computers it shows up at a size that fits within the average monitor.

Dots Per Inch (dpi) – This is the print density of the image and is the important figure. It refers to the number of pixels from the image that will appear in each inch of the printed result. In commercial printing 300dpi is used, while inkjet printers can produce decent results at anything from 150dpi upwards. It isn't worth printing at a lower dpi than this, as the result will be disappointing.

1,600x1,200 is the highest common screen resolution

Screen dpi – This refers to the number of pixels present in each inch of the screen image. You might therefore assume that whenever you change your screen resolution the screen dpi will automatically change as well, as the monitor doesn't change size. The fact that it doesn't shows that screen resolution is in control and that screen dpi only affects fonts and applications.

Screen Resolution – This is the actual number of pixels displayed on screen by your monitor. The higher it is, the more you get on screen, but the smaller everything tends to appear. Modern graphics cards are capable of producing very high resolution displays, often higher than a monitor can display. Common resolutions are 1,024x768, 1,280x1,024 and 1,600x1,200.

STEP BY STEP

RESIZING AN IMAGE

1 In the Resize dialog you can change the actual image size and set the printing size. They can be used together or independently, depending on what you want to do and the precise requirements you have. We're using the photo from the page opposite which was printed in a photographic book. Initially, the Pixel Dimensions are referred to using a percentage scale, but we can easily change this so that pixels are used instead.

2 The first thing you can do with any image is increase its size for commercial printing or just to get a bit more detail in your own printing. Be aware that this process, which is called interpolation, will make the image softer. If you increase the resolution by more than 20%, the softness may be problematic. Here we've increased the Pixel Dimensions to a width of 3,310 and because the Lock Aspect Ratio box is ticked, the height has changed accordingly.

3 The figures in the Print Size box suggest that the image is going to be enormous, but that's because the print size density is set at 72dpi. If this is altered now, it will change the image size as well. We want to set just the printing density, so untick the Resample Using box. Changing the dpi to 300 alters the print size to 10.6x7in.

4 When selected, the Resize All Layers tick box will carry out the image resizing throughout all layers present. If the Maintain Original Print Size box is ticked it will lock in place the print sizes that were present when the Resize dialog was opened. This leaves the print dpi and pixel dimensions free to be changed. As each one is altered, it will change the other accordingly. This option is useful if you know the size the image needs to be printed at to fill the page.

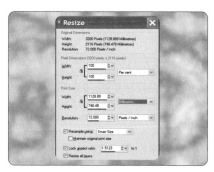

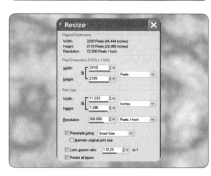

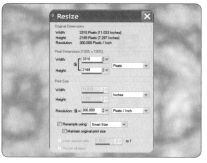

TWO THINGS AT ONCE

Be aware that the Resize option can only do two things at once in a specific order. If you change the pixel dimensions and then want to change the print size dpi, and so untick the Resample box, it will reset the pixel dimensions to their original size. You must first untick the Resample box, set the printing dpi, then tick the Resample box. You can then change the pixel dimensions.

VIDEO TUTORIAL #7

 The video tutorial demonstrates how to resize images and set the dimensions for printing.

The Crop tool

This handy tool can help change the composition of your images quickly and easily

LIMITATIONS

The Crop tool is an excellent device, but its scope is limited to cropping images so the picture centres on the subject or excludes peripheral detritus. It only lets you crop rectangularly, so it can't make clever selections for cut-outs.

Normal practice is to make a selection and crop it, which is a quick and relatively painless method that we'll explain over the page. The Crop tool, however, provides an even quicker process, has more options, and involves no pain at all. Selecting the Crop tool from the Tools toolbar activates it, and you then just draw out the area to be cropped to. If you like the shape but the positioning is slightly off, simply click and hold in the middle of the selected area, then drag it around the screen to where you want it. The handles on the midpoints and corners of the crop selection can be used to adjust the size of the selected area.

If you want to ensure that the new cropped image is the same shape as an existing one, as some aspect ratios are perfect for specific print sizes, put a tick in the Maintain Aspect Ratio box. As you mark out the area to be cropped, Paint Shop Pro keeps track of how big the new image is going to be, so that you can tell if it is still a viable resolution for printing at larger sizes. To complete the crop, simply click on the tick next to the Presets icon.

▲ **Here the Crop tool is being used to select the area for cropping**

◄ **When the Tick icon is clicked, the crop is applied**

IN DETAIL **THE CROP TOOL**

Here are the features of the Crop tool palette that appears when the tool is selected

1 This provides a list of preset sizes to crop to. It's useful, but the image resolution and print size need to be set up correctly first.

2 The Tick icon applies the crop.

3 This section shows the size of the image after the crop has taken place.

4 These four indicators show the position within the image of all four corners of the crop selection.

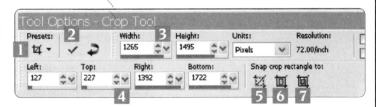

5 This icon enables you to fit the crop exactly to an existing selection in the image.

6 Click on this icon and the Crop tool snaps the selection to an image that contains transparent elements. Only the visible elements are snapped to, so you can effectively use this to select a non-square area to crop to.

7 This is similar to the previous option, but is uses all the layers to snap the selection to the outside of whatever visible material there is in any layer.

STEP BY STEP

CROPPING AN IMAGE

1 In this photograph the woman outside the ruined cathedral is too far off in the distance. The picture therefore needs cropping to bring her into the centre of the image. This needs to be done carefully because the original resolution is not very high, and too much cropping will render the picture unprintable.

2 To keep the aspect ratio of the original, we first need to select the entire image with the Crop tool, because until something is selected, the Maintain Aspect Ratio tick box is not active. If we don't make a selection that has the same aspect ratio as the image, all that clicking this box will do is preserve the ratio of the selection, not the image. In this case, this was a 3:2 aspect ratio image, so it can be cropped to a different ratio with no problems.

3 Once a crop selection has been made, you should check out what's left of the image in the Crop palette. This picture is now only 940x692 pixels which is a little on the small side. In the Image/ Resize window we've entered the value of the lowest quality of inkjet printing we can get away with – 150 ppi – to see what kind of crop is acceptable.

4 The Resolution indicator now reads 150 – changing the dimension values from pixels to inches shows what size it can be. It obviously isn't going to be much more than 7x5in so we've entered that in the Width and Height indicators. The selection of the image now changes to reflect this. The selection can then be moved to achieve the best composition. Clicking on the Tick icon carries out the crop.

RESOLUTION

Cropping causes a reduction in resolution, and resolution is king in digital images. The more pixels there are, the bigger the image can be printed. You need to judge how much interpolation can be used to bolster the cropped image and whether it will have enough pixels to print at the size you want.

The Selection tool

This collection of tools is your first port of call when marking out areas to cut, copy or process

EXTRA FEATHERING

You can turn feathering on when using the tools directly, so that as the selection is made, it is feathered. But this is just one of the options available. Leave the Feather counter at zero and instead go to Selections/ Modify. Here you'll find a host of options for feathering, increasing, contracting and smoothing the selection.

The Selection tool is actually made up of three groups of tools – Selection, Freehand Selection and Magic Wand – each with its own subset of tools. The basic Selection tool enables you to easily make rectangular, circular and elliptical selections.

The Freehand Selection tool comes with four variations – Edge Seeker, Freehand, Point to Point and Smart Edge. The Edge Seeker looks for contrasts that signify an edge, such as between land and sky. With Smart Edge, you mark a long rectangle and the program looks for the edge in it. Freehand simply lets you draw a selection for yourself. Point to Point traces around an object using straight lines that are punctuated with points inserted whenever you click the mouse.

The Magic Wand looks for pixels that are similar in colour to the one you initially click, and selects them all. You can control how closely these pixels match the initial pixel you selected – this is called the Tolerance.

The Magic Wand is ideal for selecting the sky in this picture

---

IN DETAIL SELECTION PALETTE
Here are the options available when you use the Freehand Selection tools

1 This shows the type of Freehand Selection tool being used. The options include Freehand itself, Point to Point, Edge Seeker and Smart Edge.

2 The Mode dictates how the selection is created. Here we can see the Replace mode, which creates a selection at the expense of an existing one. The other options include adding to and removing from an existing selection so that it can be tidied up.

3 The Feathering option enables you to give the selection a soft edge, determined by the value entered here.

4 This option is only available for the Edge Seeker tool. It sets how far the tool will look for significantly contrasting pixels to make the selection from.

5 The Smoothing option rounds off the edges of a selection. It's particularly useful when tracing around a curved object.

6 The Anti-alias option is a combination of feathering and smoothing, but on a small, set scale.

POINT TO POINT SELECTION

1 The Point to Point Selection tool is ideal for this kind of picture, as the edges are easy to see and the hair won't cause too many problems. With images that have blank backgrounds you'd usually use the Magic Wand, but the white background in this image would make it difficult to separate the woman from this. Select the Freehand tool and specify Point to Point. Leave Feathering at zero for now.

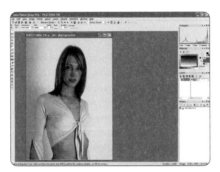

ON THE CD
Low-resolution versions of the picture of Portree on the opposite page and the model seen on this page are both on the CD, so why not try out these selection methods for yourself?

2 Zoom in to at least 100% and start by clicking at the bottom left and working your way up the outside of the arm. Click every time you want to change direction, which should be very often. Click in the joints of directional changes and remember that the more times you click and make small additions to the selection, the smoother the finished selection will be.

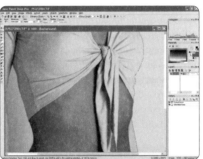

3 Go all the way around so that you end by clicking on the starting point. This should complete the initial selection. Now hold down the Control key, to switch to the mode that subtracts from the selection. The area between the arm on the left and the body contains background, so mark out that area along the edges of the figure. When you return to the original selection point for this area, it will all be removed from the selection.

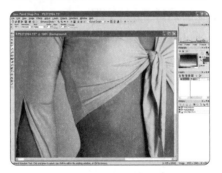

4 Use the Shift key to add to the selection where you missed bits, and the Alt key to remove any background you selected by mistake. Now go to Selections/ Modify/ Inside/Outside Feather and select Inside. Enter a value of 2 pixels and this will feather back in towards the subject, giving a softer edge. Invert the selection so the background is now selected. Pick a new colour, and using the Flood Fill tool, click on the background to replace it.

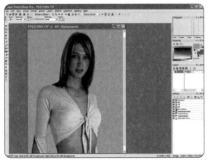

Cutting and pasting

Once you've selected part of an image you'll want to do something with it

You'll generally select a portion of an image for three reasons – because you intend to carry out a processing function on just that part, because you are going to replace it, or because you want to cut it out and use it in another composition. And that's where the Cut, Copy, Clear and Paste options come in.

The image of Portree used on page 38 has a very weak sky. Once it's been selected with the Magic Wand, the sky can be removed using the Clear option, which replaces it with the background colour. If the layer is not the Background, the selection is simply cleared and left empty. The alternative command, Cut, also removes the selected area, but places it on the Clipboard so that it can be pasted elsewhere. The Copy command makes a copy of the sky without removing it, and stores it on the Clipboard. You wouldn't want copies of this particular sky, but if the selection was inverted, the landscape could be copied and used with an alternative sky.

There is another option called Copy Merged. This works on multiple layers and copies everything that is underneath the selection, throughout the image.

If a selection is cut or cleared from a floating layer then the area selected becomes empty, showing the grid pattern for a transparent area

The area cut is rendered in the colour of the background regardless of whether the colour is set at transparent or solid in the Materials palette

PASTING OPTIONS
Selected and copied areas can be pasted in a number of ways

Paste as New Image – With this option the copied area appears in its own window as an entirely new image. The image dimensions are automatically and correctly created.
Paste as New Layer – Use this option and the area becomes an entirely new layer within the current image.
Paste as New Selection – This looks like, but isn't quite the same as, a new layer. It floats until you position it and click the mouse button, then it becomes a floating selection with content. You can clear it or modify it just as you would modify a regular selection. Or, if you want to do more with it, you can convert it into a proper layer.

Paste as Transparent New Selection – This option is the same as the previous one but with the added caveat that any pixels in the new selection that are the same colour as the background (not the background image) will be transparent.
Paste Into Selection – This means that the clipboard contents are pasted inside the selection of the existing image.
Paste as New Vector Selection – For copying and pasting vector images, where all node points need to be selected first.
Paste Animation as Multiple Images – If you have sent an animation to the clipboard, using this option makes it appear as a sequence of new images.

STEP BY STEP

PASTE IT IN

1 We're using the picture from page 39 here. The model has been flipped so she's standing the other way around. The background has been selected and a new image of a field of sunflowers has been loaded. All of this has been selected and copied to the Clipboard.

2 The model image is selected and Paste Into Selection is chosen. When pasting like this you need to be sure that the images match in terms of dimensions and orientation, as Paint Shop Pro will scale to fit regardless of the original shape.

3 This time we're going to perform the process the other way around. The selection is around the model rather than the background and the new image loaded already has a figure in it. We are going to copy the model out of one picture and into the other. To do this, click on Edit/ Copy.

4 Select the other image and go to Edit/ Paste/ Paste As New Layer. The floating image is placed on the background and can then be resized using the Deform tool. Of course, in this case you can see the original person through the gap in the arm, so this needs some attention. It is also important to remember that when matching pictures together like this, you should pay careful attention to lighting, in terms of both direction and quality.

VIDEO TUTORIAL #8

See how these pictures were put together in step by step stages.

PRINT SCREEN

There is a very useful feature in Windows called Print Screen, which is activated by pressing the appropriate key on the keyboard. This sends a copy of whatever is being displayed on the monitor to the Clipboard (rather than directly to your printer, as you might expect). Pressing Alt + Print Screen puts a copy of the active window in the Clipboard. Note that this does not tend to work very well with games, as they take over the entire Windows system.

LESSON 2
Photo montage

Try using some of the tools discussed in this chapter by following the Lesson

WHAT WILL YOU LEARN?

- How to make selections
- Saving as an alpha channel
- Saving selections to disk
- Combining images

Once you've made a complex selection, you need never do it again. You can save it as an alpha channel – a black and white mask of the selection, in which black 'blocks' pixels and white lets them through – by choosing Selections/ Load/Save Selection/ Save Selection To Alpha Channel. You can reload it later through the same menu, and either use it as a mask or convert it back into a selection (using Selections/ From Mask).

Alpha channel information is saved with the picture itself as long as you use a file format that supports this feature (such as .psp or .psd). You can also save selections straight to disk for reloading later.

Alpha channels are most useful when you're applying multiple effects to a many-layered image, or when the selection is a shape that you can use to put other pictures inside to make a design.

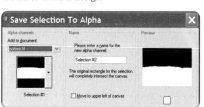

Having made a selection on the image, it has been saved to the alpha transparency channel of the native image

MORE SELECTION OPTIONS
There are yet more options to consider

Selecting – When you want to select the contents of an entire picture, press Control+A. To deselect everything, perhaps if you need to start again, press Control+D.

Matting – When you make a selection and cut something out, unless you are careful it is all too easy to leave an edge around it. With the Matting options you can trim off black, white and general edges.

Modify – After making the initial selection there are plenty of things you can do next. The selection can be expanded outwards or contracted inwards, and feathered or unfeathered. But perhaps the best part is that you can specify which way the feathering will go. Traditionally, feathering takes place on either side of the selection line, but here you can make it go outwards or inwards from the selection.

Floating – A selected area can be turned into a floating selection. This option duplicates the contents and turns it into a floating layer that can be moved and manipulated. It doesn't have a blend mode, but when there are a number of these floating layers, they can be ordered and arranged.

Promotion – A selection can be promoted to be a full, new layer. The Deform tool and other transformation tools will then work on it.

Expand...	
Contract...	
Select Similar...	
Select Colour Range...	
Feather...	Ctrl+H
Inside/Outside Feather...	
Unfeather...	
Shape Based Anti-alias...	
Recover Anti-alias...	
Remove Specks and Holes...	
Smooth...	
Select Selection Borders...	

Make more choices with your selections for better cut-outs

STEP BY STEP

COMBINING IMAGES

1 This tutorial uses the principles discussed in this chapter to replace the sky on the picture of Portree, then add in a figure. First, load all the images. Go to the Portree image and use the Magic Wand with a tolerance of 30 to add to the selection until the entire sky is selected. Go to Selections/ Modify/ Remove Specks And Holes and click on the Specks and Holes buttons. This will repair any parts of the selection that the Magic Wand has missed.

2 Now go to Selection/ Modify/ Expand and enter a value of 1. Go to Selections/ Modify/ Feather and enter a value of 2. Minimise this picture and maximise the one you will be taking the sky from. Use the Freehand selection tool to mark off the part of the sky you want, ensuring that the bottom of it is relatively straight. Press Control+C to copy it to the Clipboard then maximise the original image again.

3 Now go to Selections/ Invert so that the landscape is selected, then Edit/ Paste as New Layer to paste in the sky. Drag it up into position. Go to the landscape background layer and press Control+C to copy it. Select Paste as New Layer to drop it over the top of the sky layer in the Layers palette, and move it into position. (You may also want to use the Deform tool to squash the sky layer up a bit, as we've done here).

4 Once all this is sorted out, merge the layers down. Now bring up the portrait picture and select around the figure. Contract the selection by one pixel then feather it by one pixel. Press Control+C to copy it, switch to the scenery picture and go to Edit/ Paste/ Paste as New Layer. Select the figure and resize it with the Deform options as necessary. Merge to finish.

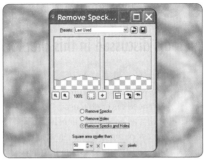

VIDEO TUTORIAL #9

Combining images can be quite tricky to master with various layer styles, which are explained more fully in the chapter on layers. Check out the tutorial first, then have a go yourself.

ON THE CD
The extra images of the Victorian lady and the sunset are on the CD, so you can use them to follow the Lesson.

CHAPTER 3
All about brushes

Applying effects, corrections and enhancements precisely is possible thanks to various brushes. In this chapter, we take a look at what they do

Selections, layers and general filters are all well and good in their place, but the real image-editing is done with the brushes. While all the tools have their own specific function, they generally stick to the same areas in the brush part of the options palette, which is what we'll look at here.

Brush tips

By 'tip' we mean the end of the brush, rather than a hint on how to use them. The brush tip can be anything from a simple feathered circle to a part of picture. The Preset icon contains the categories of brush tips, while next to it is the actual selection of tips available in that category. Often, they're subdivided into types, but you can select to see them all at once. Unlike in the previous version of Paint Shop Pro, there are only two presets for the Paintbrush now, as version 9 includes a new Art Media brush category, so everything has been divided up into new places.

Each tool type has a different collection of presets and designs, which vary from quite simple to very elaborate, depending on what the tool does. Brush tips are mainly used for painting – to paint a new image entirely or to add effects to photos. For

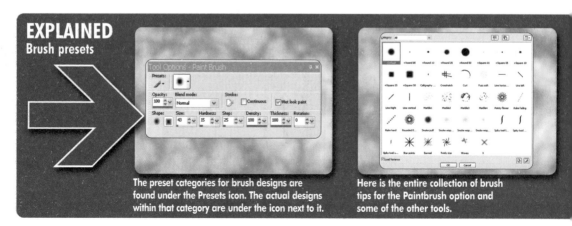

EXPLAINED
Brush presets

The preset categories for brush designs are found under the Presets icon. The actual designs within that category are under the icon next to it.

Here is the entire collection of brush tips for the Paintbrush option and some of the other tools.

that reason, the Paintbrush, Airbrush and the Art Media brushes are the most important. In one interesting option the Paintbrush uses a simulated wet-look paint, which makes it semi-transparent with thicker edges. But in terms of materials the real fun is to be had with the Art Media brushes and the Mixer palette.

Saving presets

If you want to use a brush that has particular characteristics and find that it isn't present as a default option, simply alter the existing ones to create it. You may then want to use that combination of settings on another

image. To avoid repeating yourself you can save the brush tip as a new preset. Just click on the Presets button in the Tool Options palette, enter a unique name for this brush tip and it will be saved, ready for use later.

Details change

Some tools, like the Clone Stamp, come with a set of presets but when you click on the Brush Tip Design icon, they always appear the same. What changes is not the design of the brush tips, but the details of those designs in terms of hardness, density, thickness and opacity.

ART MEDIA

As we've mentioned, the new addition to PSP in terms of brushes is Art Media. To find out more about these, turn to page 56.

If you make a change to a brush and it provides an effect you like, save it as a preset for re-use at a later date.

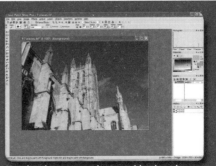

Most brushes can use the same blend modes that are found in the Layers palette. This allows specific effects to be created in target places.

VIDEO TUTORIAL #10

Selecting brushes is a piece of cake – the video tutorial shows presets and designs in action.

Brush options

Configure your brush and maximise the potential of each tool

TEXTURES
All brushes can use textures, which are split into three categories: Art Media, Geometric and Photo. They can all be scaled and rotated.

As well as altering the shape of the brush tip, there's a whole host of options to further customise the effect that you see on screen. Obviously you can paint with a solid colour, but you can also use a selection of gradients, patterns and even textures. These can be used in conjunction with the other paintbrush options to produce some very interesting effects. Although the textures aren't as effective or pronounced as a texture filter effect, they can be applied in small areas or on a specific object.

The patterns are interesting because they are a repeating design, but cleverly, it doesn't matter if you move the brush away to do something else, then come back – the pattern simply resumes at the point you were up to. It's like a scraper peeling away a white surface to reveal a pattern on the screen underneath.

How the colours, gradients, patterns and even textures are applied is dependent upon the shape of the brush tip and the settings in the Brush Options palette, so that's what we'll look at next.

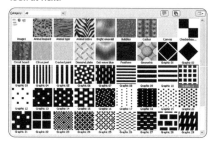

Some of the varied and interesting patterns that can be assigned to the Paintbrush

IN DETAIL BRUSH OPTIONS
Let's see what you can do with the brush once you've selected the tip

1 The two basic shapes for the brush are round and square.

2 This shows the size of the brush.

3 This affects the amount of feathering the brush has. At 100 it doesn't have any; at 1 it is very soft.

4 This shows how transparent the stroke is. At 100% opacity it is completely solid.

5 This sets how frequently the brush design is painted as you move it. If it is set to 1 it will appear every pixel; if it's at 50 then there will be a gap between dabs.

6 The same Blend Modes that are available for layers can be used for brushes.

7 The Density sets how many pixels will be used in the brush stroke. At 100% all of them will be used – a lower figure will create gaps in the stroke.

8 This sets how thin or thick the brush is. With a high number it is as wide as it is high. With a low number it is like a traditional paintbrush, long and thin.

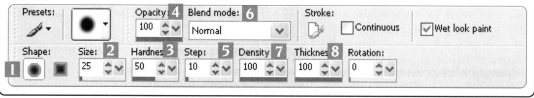

STEP BY STEP

CREATING A CUSTOM BRUSH

1 When creating your own brushes, the first point to note is that they are in a greyscale format – ie shades of grey from white to black. This sets how the paint is applied – the blacker the part of the custom brush, the stronger it will appear. Create a new image at 250x250 pixels and select the Paintbrush and black ink. Pick a standard circular brush and enter 11 in the Size box.

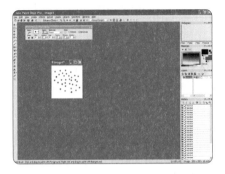

2 Puts some dots all over the little image then reduce the brush opacity to 50% and add a few more. Go to File/ Export/ Custom Brush. Enter a name for your brush, along with your name as the creator and then decide how often you want the pattern to repeat when painting with it. A value of 1 will just draw lines, so enter 8 for a real scatter-gun effect. Click OK.

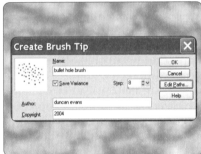

3 Load an image to draw on, or create a blank one. Go to the Shapes icon in the Tool Options palette when the Paintbrush is selected. In amongst all the other brushes you should now see your own. Double-click on it to start using it.

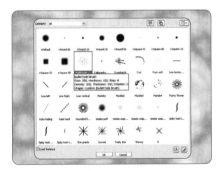

4 The brush will then appear in the Tool Options palette and you can change any of the variables that are applicable. As this brush consists of dots it doesn't have a hardness or thickness variant, but you can easily create your own brushes that are more solid and so will have these characteristics. By altering the brush size you can now create quite different effects, from noticeably dotty with a 250 pixel size, to a more scratchy effect at 50.

BRUSH LIMITATIONS
The maximum size for a brush in Paint Shop Pro is 500x500 pixels. All brushes are saved in greyscale format using the PSP brush format.

The Warp brush

Go mad with freehand distortion effects using the Warp brush

AIRBRUSH
This is the same as in PSP 8. It builds the spray up, but lacks the variety and depth that natural media-specific tools have, which would make it more realistic.

This hasn't changed much since the last version of Paint Shop Pro, and it's not really a particularly serious tool. The Warp brush has a similar function to some of the Deform tools, but does it in a freehand fashion. As such it's not entirely practical because if you need to make little adjustments it's safer to use the Smudge brush, and if you need large-scale manipulation with some accuracy then the Deform tools are better suited to the task.

Basically, the Warp brush moves pixels around, compresses them or expands them. As such it's rather like that other well-known face-altering software, Goo. It enables you to make people look as freakish as your twisted desires demand, by pushing areas into each other, sucking them in, or blowing them out, like an explosion of pixels. Because this tool is so

destructive you can cancel the effect or click on the Tick button to apply it, meaning you can experiment in safety.

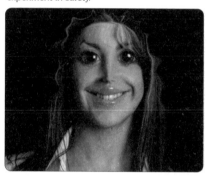

This young lady won't thank us for this, but the Push option was used to crimp the hair, the Expand option produced great bug eyes, and the Contract option allowed us to shrink the nose

IN DETAIL **THE WARP BRUSH TOOL**
Check out this madcap tool's modes and options

1 Using this icon you can apply or cancel the effects you've just applied in one Warp mode.

2 The Push function works like the Smudge tool.

3 This expands pixels outwards...

4 ...And this sucks them in like water down a drain.

5 This creates a random pixel-displacement effect.

6 The Size and Hardness options are exactly the same as with the other brush tools. The Strength specifies how strong the effect is.

7 The Background Mode dictates how the pixel shoving will work.

8 Reduce the Draft Quality to speed things up if you need to experiment first. Then you can apply the effect at top quality when you're happy with it.

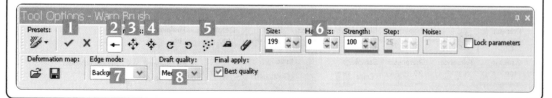

Background Eraser

When you're finding making a selection difficult, use this tool instead

There are occasions when you want to replace the background but the foreground simply covers too much of it, leaving numerous isolated pockets – like the sky through trees, for example. This makes using the Magic Wand or Freehand Selection tool either plainly impractical or too laborious to make it worth your while. This is where the Background Eraser comes in. It samples a point when you click the mouse, and erases everything of a similar colour as you make brushstrokes through the image. There are various ways in which you can get the best out of this tool.

One of the most significant choices you'll make is whether to use Auto Tolerance detection or enter a figure yourself. The problem with setting the program to automatic is that it isn't infallible and can end up erasing the foreground

as well as the background. Setting a custom tolerance figure yourself allows you to judge the difference between the foreground and background and adjust it accordingly – you may need to resample as you go along though.

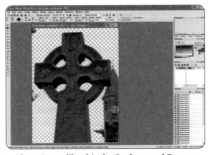

With a picture like this the Background Eraser comes into its own, as the foreground objects are very different in colour and brightness

BEST USE
The ideal image to use this tool on is one with a background that is significantly different in terms of brightness and colour. It might also be fragmented by the foreground, making selection problematic.

IN DETAIL **BACKGROUND ERASER**
Use the right settings to avoid rubbing out the entire picture

1 The size dictates how much you can rub out at once.

2 The Tolerance sets the variation in pixels from the selected colour. A high figure may erase the foreground; a low figure might not erase all the background.

3 This determines how feathered the edge of the eraser is when removing the background.

4 With the Once option, when you click the first time that will be the sampled colour you use until you release the mouse button and click again.

5 The Contiguous option means the pixels have to be connected – if there is a distinct border on a foreground image, any colours on the other side of it will not be erased even if they are the right colour.

6 Use this option to leave Paint Shop Pro to work out the tolerance, or turn it off and enter the value yourself.

7 If the image has multiple layers, this option will merge them to generate a final pixel colour for use as the sample.

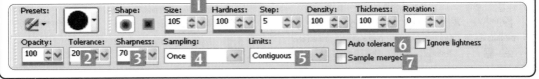

The Clone tool

One of the most important tools in the digital photographer's armoury

SCRATCH REMOVER

The alternative to the Clone tool is the Scratch Remover. This uses the same technology as the Clone tool, and attempts to repair small scratches, usually in scanned film, by filling in from either side. It's largely automatic but is a useful option.

The Clone tool basically copies pixels from a sampled area and paints them into the target area. This makes it an ideal tool for removing objects from photo.

Ever taken a picture of an olde worlde street in some sleepy hamlet and despaired at the television aerials on the roofs? With the Clone tool you can remove them, replacing the area with sky. The trick with the Clone tool is to avoid making the area that you replace look false, by suddenly changing shade or using patterns from the sample area that then repeat. Repeated patterns are instantly noticeable and will give away your digital shenanigans. To set the area you wish to copy from, simply move the cursor to that point and press the right mouse button. You can then clone away by pressing the left button.

There are three key options to consider when using the Clone tool – the Hardness, the Opacity, and the Blend Mode. These can be used in different ways to create a variety of different effects.

A telephone cable cuts across the corner of this photo, and near the bottom a spire protrudes into the picture. The Clone tool can be used to remove both fairly easily

IN DETAIL THE CLONE TOOL

Discover the important elements of this crucial tool

1 This shows the size of the brush. The larger the brush the bigger the area that can be cloned at once.

2 The Hardness sets the brush's level of feathering.

3 The Opacity is a key function. At 100% it copies everything, while at lower opacities it is more subtle.

4 The Blend Mode affects how the copied pixels are painted onto the picture. You'll probably want to make use of at least two other modes besides Normal.

5 If this box is ticked, after you have cloned one area the next cloning action will use a sampled area that is in the same relative position as the target area that was initially set. If it isn't ticked, then on every subsequent mouse click, the sampled area resets to the initial area chosen.

6 If there are multiple layers in the image and this option is ticked, PSP will perform a calculation to work out what the merged results of the layers would be for the sampling area.

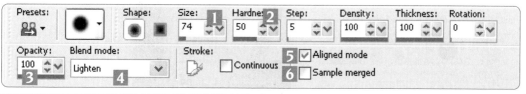

Presets:		Shape:	Size: **1**	Hardnes **2**	Step:	Density:	Thickness:	Rotation:
			74	50	5	100	100	0

Opacity:	Blend mode:	Stroke:	
100 **3**	Lighten **4**	☐ Continuous	**5** ☑ Aligned mode **6** ☐ Sample merged

STEP BY STEP

CLONE IT OUT

1 Zoom in to the face to at least 100% so that you have a good clear view of what is going on. There are a number of spots, moles and hairs on this face that need to be tackled. Click on the Clone tool and set the Blend Mode to Lighten. Leave the Opacity at 100% for now and pick a feathered brush. If you can't decide whether the brush is feathered or not, pick any and set the Hardness to 50.

2 Set the Blend Mode to Lighten. Now any pixels in the target area that are darker than ones in the sampled area will be replaced. This allows you to remove blemishes on the skin, avoiding an obvious circular pattern but retaining the sharpness and texture. However, the skin tones used must be the same and you should avoid sampling too close to the target area or a pattern may emerge. First, try removing the hair on the forehead, then the blemish below it.

3 The growth to the left of the top of the nose has lighter and darker elements. The Blend Mode will therefore need to be set to Lighten for the first pass and Darken for the second. Darken works just like Lighten, but the opposite way round. If the source area is darker than the target area, the darker pixels will be copied. You can also use this mode to erase blemishes like scars.

4 To get rid of the dimple marks by each corner of the mouth, change the Blend Mode to Lighten and set the Opacity to 35%. Sample from all around these areas to remove the shadows. If a lighter area needs joining up to the other areas, switch the Blend Mode to Normal and reduce the Opacity to 20%. This will allow you to merge the areas together.

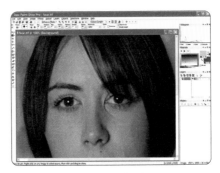

VIDEO TUTORIAL #11

There is a real art to successful cloning that comes with practice and an innate ability to see the patterns and ways in which the problems can be solved. Watch the video to see this in action then have a go yourself – a lower-resolution version of the picture used here is provided on the CD for you to practice with.

Photo brushes

Use these tools to make precise spot adjustments to your photos

HSL ADJUSTMENT
There is also a set of brush tools dedicated to Hue, Saturation and Brightness spot adjustments, and for copying colour.

There are seven tools grouped together under the Dodge tool, most of which are designed for making spot adjustments to photos. The most useful are Dodge, which makes things less intense, and Burn, which makes them more intense – it isn't just a case of being brighter or darker. These tools can make objects in shadow more prominent, or make clouds stand out in the sky. Smudge is for smearing and Push is for shoving pixels; Soften blends things into the background, and Sharpen makes them more distinct. (Use Sharpen with great care as it can cause severe pixelation). Finally, the Emboss tool is great for giving parts of your photo a brass-rubbing effect.

Most of these tools replicate the effects of filters, but are useful in that they can be applied selectively and mixed at will. We recommend you create a duplicate layer to work on – that way, if the effect is too strong, you can reduce the opacity of the layer.

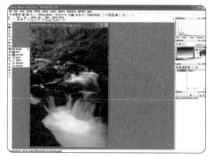

The Dodge and Burn tools can be used to make areas more or less intense. Here, the water can be made brighter and the rocks darker

IN DETAIL DODGE & BURN
Set the parameters carefully to use these tools effectively

1 This shows the size of the brush. A large feathered brush is ideal for items like clouds – a smaller one might leave a noticeable trail.

2 The Hardness sets the level of feathering the brush uses. You'll usually want these tools to use a feathered brush.

3 The Density value sets which of the pixels in the brush shape will work. It is of no real use with Dodge and Burn, but could have some effect when using the Smear tool.

4 Rotation applies to brushes that are a specific shape, rather than just round. It rotates them, obviously.

5 The Opacity sets the strength of the tool and is a very important value. Anything above 5% will have a strong, noticeable effect. At 5% or under the effect is very subtle.

6 The Limit option sets the tonal range used. The range includes Shadows, Midtones, Highlights and None, which means all tones.

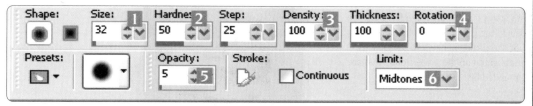

STEP BY STEP

DODGE & BURN

1 The dominance of reflective white tones in this image means the camera's metering system was fooled into under-exposing it. That's good news for us because it means there are plenty of things to correct. The snow needs to be whiter, while the clouds can be made far more threatening.

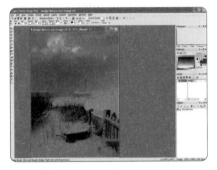

VIDEO TUTORIAL #12

Watch how the Dodge and Burn tools are used on this image, then have a go yourself – the picture is on the CD.

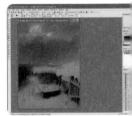

2 Select the Dodge tool and pick a decent sized brush (say 100) that has a nicely feathered edge (use a Hardness of 50). Set the Opacity to 10% and the Limits to Midtones. Apply expansive strokes to the snowy areas. This is a high opacity setting but because there is a lot of snow, and it's all the same kind of tone, there is no need to be conservative. Even so, it may take a few coats to get the lower garden to the right brightness.

3 Select the Burn Tool and set the Opacity to 5%. Use the same general brush tones, but change the Limits to None. Have a go at painting the sky in circular motions that follow the formations of cloud. Up at the top, aim to go around the slightly clear patch so that the white clouds are surrounded by dark, snow-laden ones. The aim is not to make everything dark but to provide definition.

4 Now we need to work on the ruined croft house. Set the Burn tool to 10% and the brush size to 50 and make the walls stand out. Do the same for the fence posts in the garden. Switch back to the Dodge tool and change it to 5% Opacity, then brighten up the white clouds that are surrounded by the storm clouds.

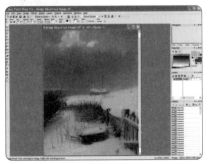

The Deform tools

Rotate images, resize on the fly and correct converging with the Deform tools

AVOID VERTICALS
To avoid converging verticals in the first place, and save yourself the effort of having to correct them later with the Deform tools, use a specialist camera with a shift lens or stand well back and zoom in with a long lens.

There are four Deformation tools – Deform, Straighten, Perspective Correction and Mesh Warp. Idiosyncratically, they're available as tools rather than through drop-down menus, but unlike all the other tools, which use brushes, these are selection- or purely image-based. The Straighten and Perspective Correction tools might appear to duplicate options available within the Deform tool, but both offer more control and variety when offered as tools in their own right.

The Deform tool has four modes of operation: Scale, Perspective, Free and Shear. Scale is the easiest to use, as it simply resizes the image along the horizontal and vertical axis. The Perspective mode makes the top of the image appear to fall away by decreasing it in size, or

come towards you by increasing it in size. The Shear mode makes the image slide one way or the other. The Free mode allows you to move all corners in any direction, and the image is then distorted accordingly.

Go mad with the Deform tool. This tool in itself it has four modes of operation

MESH WARP
Plot your co-ordinates carefully to apply a warping process with some precision

Well, when we say precision we mean in comparison to the Warp brush, which is just insanity on a long wooden stick!

Predictably, the Mesh Warp tool puts a mesh over the image, the rows and columns of which can be set. The more there are, the more subtle the effects will be, but the more tweaking you have to do. Essentially, the direction you move the control points in dictates where the pixels will be pushed, meaning you can expand or compress areas at will. A draft version is shown on screen so you can see what's going on. If you have a slow computer the draft quality can be reduced to speed it up, but it should be plenty fast enough.

One of the main advantages of the Mesh Warp tool is that it not only allows you to save specific patterns of the warp map, but to load those supplied with PSP as well. These offer a variety of interesting effects.

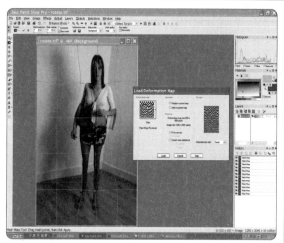

You can save the warp meshes you create or load a variety of designs that come with PSP – it was too late to save this girl though

STEP BY STEP

PERSPECTIVE CORRECTION

1 The term 'converging verticals' is used to describe a photographed building that appears to be falling backwards or in on itself. It happens because of lens distortion and the angle of light entering the camera when shooting. As a result, a wide-angle lens makes things much worse. Load the picture and make the window as large as possible, but zoom out so there's plenty of space to manipulate the handles.

2 Select the Deform tool and choose the Perspective mode. This has one advantage over the Perspective Correction tool – it shows you a live preview. The bad news is that as you adjust one side, the handle on the other side of the image moves as well. Grab hold of the top-left handle and move it up slightly and to the left. Pull down the bottom left one a little. That should give a reasonable, but not perfect, result.

3 Alternatively, use the Perspective Correction tool. This has its advantages but a few bad points too. The advantages are that you can specify a number of grid lines and that the control points can be moved independently. The disadvantages are that the grid doesn't cover the entire image and there is no preview. Helpfully though, you can line up the lines of the grid with the current verticals in the image.

4 There is an option to crop the image once it's been deformed, but as you don't know the result prior to applying it, it is better to crop manually at the end of the process when the result is satisfactory. Normally though, it's pretty good – often, all that is then required is either to crop or slightly compress it if it's been stretched vertically too much.

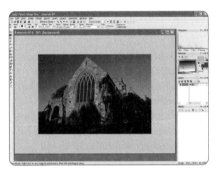

EXTREME CORRECTION

For really bad verticals you may need to run the Deform correction process twice. Click on the Reset icon to return the grid to its original starting position so that it can be manipulated again.

ON THE CD
The picture of the church is on the CD so you can practise straightening verticals.

Art Media brushes

Let your creativity run wild with a selection of natural media brushes

CONFUSED ABOUT ART?
If you try to paint on a Background layer, PSP will automatically create a blank Art Media layer. When you attempt to use the regular Eraser on the Art Media layer, PSP will convert the layer to a Raster layer to make it work.

The new Art Media brush set offers six brush types (Oil Brush, Chalk, Pastel, Crayon, Coloured Pencil and Marker) and three tools to use with them (Palette Knife, Smear and Art Eraser). Oils are a wet media, so when they're painted over each other in different colours, they blend. Chalk, Pastel and Crayon work similarly to one another. The Coloured Pencil is like a regular brush but with a lower density value, so there's a little trail of unpainted pixels in it. The Marker Pen gives a similar result to a brush, until you draw over it again, at which point the ink becomes darker where the lines cross.

The Palette Knife is half tool, half brush. Load the triangular knife with paint and you'll find that as you apply it, it quickly runs out. The Smear tool scrapes paint from one area to another, but as it has no strength settings its use is limited. Finally, the Art Eraser does the same as the Eraser, but without any fine control.

Here's Oil Brush at work making use of the Trace option, which samples and uses the colour that is under the brush at the start of the stroke

IN DETAIL **THE OIL BRUSH**
It's the most interesting of the Art Media brushes, so let's see how it works

1 The Presets icon holds a variety of different brush tips.

2 The Thickness is important because of the Head Tracking option. It sets how long and thin the brush is.

3 The Rotation tilts long and thin brushes. Obviously, it has no effect with round brushes.

4 Once again, with a circular brush this doesn't mean anything, but for proper artist brush shapes it can be fixed in position to follow the direction the cursor goes in.

5 This sets how much paint is loaded onto the brush, which determines the coverage before it runs dry.

6 This is how fluid the paint is. A more fluid paint runs and mixes, while a less fluid paint is stodgy.

7 This sets how stiff the brush is and whether it bends as you paint.

8 The Clean options offer a choice of methods for wiping the brush clean.

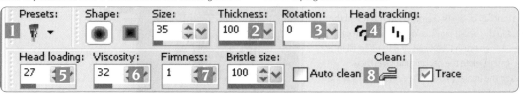

OILS IN ACTION

1 It has to be said that using a graphic pen and tablet makes this kind of tool much easier to use. It's not easy simulating brush strokes with a mouse. So, while the pen brigade can quite happily repaint landscapes, if you are a mouse user, large-detail pictures make this easier. In this case, we're talking about a close-up portrait. Select the Oil Brush and use the Preset options to pick the Bristle Old Clumped brush.

2 Reduce the brush size to 20 and the Head loading to 15, then zoom in to 100%. Tick the Trace box and start with the hair, making strokes that follow it. Merge them together as you progress along. When tackling the blonde highlights in the hair, remember to click on the Clean icon first, otherwise they will be brown rather than blonde. For bits of hair that stick out of the head, follow them through with long strokes until the paint runs out.

3 Change to a 40 pixel brush and switch Auto Clean on for the face. Use small dabs in the directions that the angles run in. So, the nose would be down, the cheeks sideways, the jawline diagonal, and the chin would require circular motion. Increase the brush size to 50 for the neck and shoulders as this requires the least detail. The neck should run sideways then downwards. Set the brush size back to 30 and go over the neck areas again.

4 For the eyes and the area around them, set the brush size to 10 and turn on Auto Clean. Turn Auto Clean off for the lips, but clean the brush before doing the teeth. Now turn off the visibility of the Background layer to reveal the gaps in the background, select the Smear tool with a large brush (75 pixels), and use it to fill in the gaps. Delete the background layer then flatten the image to place the Art layer on a white background.

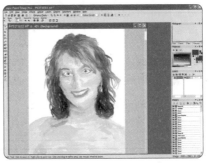

TAKING IT FURTHER
Obviously, space is limited here, but you could go on to make this image more realistic through the use of filters and textured backgrounds.

ON THE CD
This portrait is on the CD, so you can splash paint all over it to your heart's content..

LESSON 3
Clean complexions

Use the array of tools at your command to spruce up someone's appearance

STEP BY STEP

GET CLEANING

1 Zoom in to 150%, so that you can really see what you're doing on the forehead. Select the Clone tool with Opacity of 100% and change the Blend Mode to Lighten. Select a brush with a feathered edge. If it does not have one set, change the Hardness to 50. Sample from the side of the spot, looking for an area of skin that will be the same tone as the area you are rectifying. Right-click to set the sample zone and left-click to use it.

2 Now let's attack the pimples on the rest of the face. The Lighten Blend Mode works by comparing the sample area with the target area – if the sample pixels are lighter than the target pixels, it replaces them. As spots are darker, you can replace them with normal skin, without producing a large circular shape that would result from a straightforward clone of an area.

3 To remove the lines under the eyes and any variance in skin tone, switch the Opacity to 20% and the Blend Mode to Normal. Sample from just under the eyes and sweep upwards, avoiding obvious edges. Work on reasonably-sized areas to avoid creating just one slightly smooth patch. After a few strokes you may start to see repeating patterns, so change the sample position relative to the cursor and work over it again. Don't rework areas too much, just do enough to fade the lines out.

W ith just a few tools you can really improve someone's appearance. Using the Clone and Dodge tools you can remove spots and blemishes, whiten eyes and give teeth a good old polish.

STEP BY STEP

4 Now we'll work on the nose. Change the Opacity to 10% and shrink the brush. Avoiding the nostrils and any obvious boundaries, smooth out red blemishes. Then, using a big brush with the Opacity at 20%, remove the smile lines. Keep your sampling areas below the cheek as this is a slightly different colour to the middle. However the cheek on the right needs to be extended down into the line area and met from below.

5 Select the Dodge tool and choose a 5 pixel brush. Set the Opacity to 20% and zoom in to 200%. Carefully paint over the whites of the eyes to make them brighter. Next, use a very small Clone brush on obvious veins. If there is a colour cast in either eye, select the Saturation Up/Down brush. Set the size to 5% and the Opacity to 35%, then, using the right mouse button, wipe the area until it looks whiter. Then use the Dodge brush to make it lighter.

6 Move on to the teeth now with the Dodge brush and use the same principles. If some teeth are yellow rather than just dull-looking, increase the Opacity of the Saturation Up/Down brush to 40% to reduce this. Teeth normally suffer from some kind of discolouration unless the owner has had expensive treatment. Run the Saturation brush over all of them using the right mouse button.

7 Finally, use a small 5 pixel brush at an Opacity of 20% and the Clone tool to smooth out any lipstick. Zoom in to 250 or 300% for precise work. Next, select a much bigger brush (about 30 pixels), set the Blend Mode to Lighten and the Opacity to 50% and remove things like creases in the neck and strap marks on the shoulders. Set the Blend Mode back to Normal and reduce the Opacity to 20% to blend these areas in with the surrounding ones.

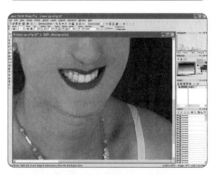

VIDEO TUTORIAL #13

 In the video tutorial the Clone tool is used with the Blend Mode set to Lighten to clean up a complexion.

CHAPTER 4

Photographic tools

Digital cameras are the must-have tool of the 21st century, especially as prices continue to drop. PSP 9 welcomes them onboard

There are two main reasons why people buy and use Paint Shop Pro. One is to create images, either for Web use or for artistic purposes. The other reason is for correcting, enhancing and printing their digital camera pictures. Jasc has taken this on board in version 9 and has provided a number of new tools and filters to apply to your digital photos.

We'll start by looking at the common bugbears of digital camera use – digital noise and chromatic aberration, or colour fringing. Then there are the automatic functions that tackle contrast, colour and saturation. A number of new cameras now offer the AdobeRGB 1998 Color Space Specification, but most before that were limited to sRGB, which provided a much more restricted colour gamut (range of colours). As a result digital images never had much colour or contrast. Cameras that did try to ramp up the colour saturation usually only succeeded in creating ghastly hues of verdant foliage and florid skin tones.

The exposure meter can often get its job wrong. The resulting problems are tackled with the Fill Flash and Backlighting filters. The Levels and Curves controls will also do the job, but you need to know how

DISCOVER IN THIS CHAPTER

Tackle coloured digital noise problems caused by high digital ISO ratings or long exposure.

Use the automatic tools as a quick fix for photos. They can resolve problems with colour, add more contrast and increase the saturation.

to apply them. We show you how in one of the following sections of the book as well as in a video tutorial.

Soft pictures

Digital camera users have also learned to accept soft pictures, due partly to the fact that the camera only has a limited ability to make a good job of sharpening images. Sharpening, or apparent sharpening, is best done on the computer, which is where Unsharp Mask and the Sharpen commands come in. Use them wisely and your images will be sharp and punchy – get it wrong and they will be badly pixelated. We

provide you with a step-by-step tutorial to using the Unsharp Mask, and further back it up with a video guide.

We also look at correcting distortion, which can even be caused by high-quality SLR lenses, not just the inexpensive lenses on digital compact cameras. We'll demonstrate some general enhancements you can make, rounding the chapter off with a lesson on typical photo-correction techniques. We'll bring you much more on photo correction techniques in a future issue of PSP Library that will be dedicated to digital image editing and enhancement projects.

BRUSH LIMITATIONS

Birds are difficult to capture without a very expensive lens. The above picture is therefore overexposed and a little blurred. In this chapter we'll show you how to make it look sharper and give it more punch.

Learn how to use Levels and Curves to correct badly exposed pictures, or to enhance the tonality of reasonable but unremarkable images.

The Curves tool can enhance all areas of the image, including shadow detail and how bright the highlights appear.

VIDEO TUTORIALS

There are three video tutorials in this chapter. These look at sharpening pictures, making tonal adjustments and creatively blurring parts of the image.

Noise removal

Undue noise is the bane of the digital photographer's life

REDUCING NOISE
Use the lowest ISO setting possible to reduce the chances of your picture suffering from coloured digital noise. On long exposures some cameras have a noise-reduction function.

Digital cameras sometimes generate coloured noise. When they're set at higher digital ISO ratings, they read the light from the CCD more quickly and therefore less accurately. As a result, fluctuation in light becomes speckles of coloured light.

Yet when the light is falling and flash is inappropriate, what can you do but ramp up the ISO? Well, you're supposed to try a long exposure. But whereas it becomes difficult to judge the exposure for film in low light, digital reacts differently. Instead of being super-saturated, colours come out dark and bland, and blocks of similar-coloured noise (usually green) appear in bands in the dark areas of the image.

This is where PSP's new noise-removal tool comes in. This provides two windows: in one you can define the areas to sample; in the other you can pan slowly around the image. Clicking anywhere in the former window adds a new sample rectangle – to remove it, grab its handles and resize it to zero.

This long exposure produced lots of noise in the shadowed areas and in the orange of the sunset

---

IN DETAIL NOISE REMOVAL
Find your way around this tool to effectively reduce digital noise

1 This is a sample area that has been defined and placed over an area of noise in the picture.

2 This is the panning window. Grab the image shown here to move around the view in both windows.

3 Use this tab to protect a range of colours from the process, ensuring that detail won't be lost in areas that don't suffer from noise.

4 The correction tool attacks different types of noise. High ISO noise is small while long exposure noise is large. Change the settings here to reflect the noise in your image.

5 This determines how much the colours adjacent to the noise blend together. A higher figure removes more noise but makes the picture softer...

6 ...Which is why this option is provided to try to sharpen it again. Rather than use it, we suggest you run PSP's sharpening processes yourself.

7 The overall picture window shows where the sample areas are located. Unfortunately, you can't simply click on them and move them.

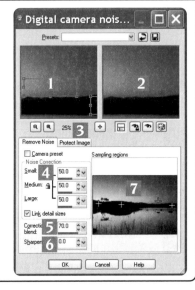

Chromatic aberration

The curse of cheap lenses and unforgiving skies is chromatic aberration

NEW FOR PSP9

Chromatic aberration is rarer on film cameras than on digital cameras, and digital compacts are more prone to the problem than SLRs. Quality of lens is one reason for this, but there is another. Most digital cameras use a matrix of red, green (x2) and blue elements for each block of four diodes or pixels in the image – so there is only a one in four chance that the red or blue colours will be detected correctly, and a 50-50 chance that the green colour will be picked. While this sounds appalling, the problem only occurs with mixed-colour objects and at the edges of objects that are the same colour. The firmware in cameras is designed to identify surfaces, objects and textures, and process the colour matrix accordingly. However, this breaks down at the edge of dark objects framed by white skies. Because the

transition from one area to another is sudden and contrasts so completely, the firmware can interpret this wrongly and put blue in on one side of the object and red-brown on the other side. Paint Shop Pro 9, however, has a filter that can help.

A glaring white-sky day means chromatic aberration was certain to happen

MINIMISING ABERRATION
While to some extent there's nothing you can do about chromatic aberration, if the conditions are such that they are going to make it worse, avoid taking shots of things with a prominent sky, or of vertical constructs set against the sky.

IN DETAIL CHROMATIC ABBERATION CORRECTION
This is an incredibly effective filter that can make a big difference with little effort

1 This is a sample area that you define on the original image in this window. Mark it around an area that contains chromatic aberration.

2 This is the sample window. You can't move this window around unless you click on the cross icon centred below the two windows.

3 However, if you move your mouse over this window it changes to a hand icon and you can move it around to find the next area to sample.

4 The list of the sample areas you have marked out appears here.

5 This shows the colour range in the sample area that you have selected. If you find you are losing colour elsewhere, look for it in the samples and remove that one.

6 Alternatively, you can alter this setting, which is the opacity of the cleaning effect based on the sample areas.

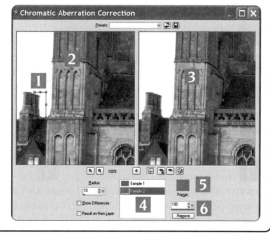

Auto Colour, Contrast

Correct the colour and tonal characteristics of your image, instantly

COLOUR TEMPERATURE
All light has a colour temperature that gives off a particular colour cast and is rated in terms of degrees Kelvin. The light of a sunny day at noon is generally thought to be 6,500K. Light with a higher colour temperature is bluer, and light with a lower temperature (like artificial lamps and sunset) is redder.

Paint Shop Pro 9 has a one-click feature for correcting all your slightly off photos – the One Step Photo Fix. This feature applies colour balance, saturation and contrast enhancement tools, as well as the Edge Preserving Smooth filter, to your picture. This last filter isn't really very suitable for landscape shots. The alternative to the One Step option is to use a range of three separate tools to tackle colour balance, contrast and saturation.

Automatic Colour Balance is set up to counter colour casts caused by Automatic White Balance that either hasn't done its job, or has done it too well. It can be used to warm pictures or to restore the natural blues if the colour is too red-brown. Automatic Contrast Enhancement provides some easy ways to

boost contrast, which don't involve simply altering the contrast slider. Automatic Saturation Enhancement boosts colours, while preserving skin tones.

This shot was taken on a sunny day, but the camera has produced a picture with weak colours and a lack of contrast, and has failed to capture the real blueness of the sky and water

---

IN DETAIL AUTOMATIC COLOUR BALANCE

Tweak the Colour Balance to amend any inaccuracies in digital camera Automatic White Balance

1 This window shows the original picture and colours.

2 Here you can see the results of the colour balance operation. The image can be grabbed and moved around to show areas out of the window's range.

3 The Strength sets how powerful the colour correction will be. If you find other parts of the image are being affected, you may want to reduce this.

4 Ticking this allows you to remove a strong colour cast in the picture.

5 This is the engine of the process, where you set the colour temperature of the conditions when the picture was shot. As this picture was shot at mid-day in blue skies, it's almost exactly 6,500K. When selected, this returned plenty of blue to the picture but gave the beach a red tinge.

6 There are a number of Presets here for the differing conditions in which the picture may have been taken.

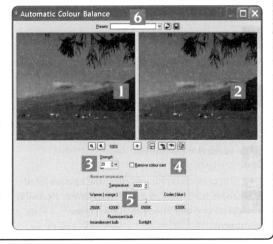

and Saturation

IN DETAIL AUTOMATIC CONTRAST ENHANCEMENT
Give your pictures that quick fix boost without risking highlights

1 The style of this process is much like that of Automatic Colour Balance, and indeed most PSP processes. This window displays the actual photo, showing how much or how little contrast is present.

2 Adjacent to it is this preview window, which you can pan around so that you can check individual areas. You can also zoom out to see the whole picture.

3 This sets whether you want the image to be brighter, the same or darker.

4 The Strength section only provides two options – the Mild setting is a weak version of the Normal setting.

5 This is where the contrast is altered. Flat reduces the

contrast, Natural keeps it the same and Bold enhances it. This latter option usually makes parts of the picture darker as well.

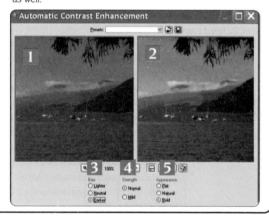

IN DETAIL AUTOMATIC SATURATION ENHANCEMENT
Pump up the colour volume with Automatic Saturation Enhancement

1 OK, so you know what this window does by now – it's the original image. You can move it around if you click on the little cross icon.

2 Again, this is the preview window. If you resize the entire dialog, a bigger preview window can be gained without zooming in or out.

3 These zoom into or out of the image.

4 The Less Colourful option reduces saturation, the Normal one leaves it as it is, while the More Colourful option increases the saturation.

5 This controls how much effect the options listed above have. Weak is a small adjustment, Normal is a moderate one and Strong is a large colour adjustment.

6 When this is ticked, saturation enhancements will not be applied to skin tones. You can therefore avoid making your subjects look pale and mysterious, or like they're fresh from the tropics after forgetting the sun cream.

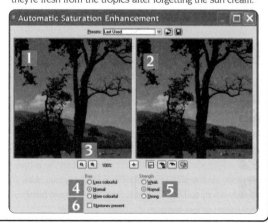

Fill Flash Filter

Portrait cursed by a bright background, leaving your subject in shadow? Read on...

FILL IT IN
If your camera doesn't have a fill in flash mode and you are shooting with the sun behind the subject, just use a regular flash.

BOUNCE BACK
The alternative to using a flash is to use a reflector to bounce light back at the subject. A big sheet of white card will do the job.

This is the portrait photographer's sneaky top tip for shooting subjects that have bright light behind them. It balances the exposure so that you get a perfect foreground and background. It's also used on overcast days when there is little light falling on the subject's face, or if the sun is overhead and ugly shadows would result. The fill in flash lightens the face and cancels out all the shadows.

PSP's filter tries to do something similar, but it isn't intelligent – it can't determine where the person is in the picture, so it simply lightens all the dark tones in the image, regardless of what or where they are. This is fine if the background isn't too bright to start with. If the person is well exposed but the background is too light, use the Backlighting Filter instead.

The subject is lit by strong sunlight from behind and this has affected the exposure metering

IN DETAIL FILL FLASH FILTER
This new PSP 9 feature is designed to replicate a real portrait technique

1 This is the original picture, showing that the subject is backlit and so is rendered in shadow.

2 The live preview window allows you to pan around the image. You can see that the effect used has lightened the subject very well. However, this has also spilled over, causing most of the left-hand side to lack contrast and the car behind to become lighter.

3 The Zoom buttons show the effect more closely.

4 When the Preview Window button is pressed both the original and the working preview windows appear. You can turn them off, though that rather defeats the point.

5 When clicked on, the Auto Proof button updates the main image with the settings, allowing you to have the dialog window quite small.

6 Performs a one-off preview using the main image.

7 This controls the strength of the filter. Check to see if the figure is light enough and whether the spill into the background has had a detrimental effect.

Backlighting Filter

Another new PSP 9 feature to doff its cap at digital photography is the Backlighting Filter

Closely related to the Fill Flash Filter is the Backlighting Filter. It works on the premise that the metering was optimised for the figures in the foreground and, as a result, the landscape in the background is either over-exposed or just very bright. To use this filter on a picture, the subject or foreground should be properly exposed as they may be affected by it. It works by simply making the very light tones darker. If that includes the face or, more likely, light clothing like a white T-shirt, then expect it to be affected and become darker when it might have been fine to start with. If the balancing act between the subject and the background is proving too difficult, we suggest you use the Curves function.

The foreground figures are OK but the background is very bright due to the sun burning through a shroud of sea fog then blazing off the waves

DIFFICULT CONDITIONS
The Fill Flash and the Backlighting filters are designed to correct one aspect of the photo and assume that the other is fine. If that isn't the case, then use Levels or Curves, possibly with an Adjustment layer mask.

IN DETAIL BACKLIGHTING FILTER
Correct bright backgrounds with this easy-to-use filter

1 This is a very simple filter and effect, so there are no presets for it beyond using the last-used setting.

2 The ability to save the settings as a Preset is here more for the sake of conformity with other dialogs than because it's of much practical value.

3 This window shows the sand, sea, and sky have all been toned down by the filter, without affecting the subjects.

4 The Randomise function selects the parameters to use at, well, random. As there is only one in this filter, you probably won't find this to be of much use!

5 The Strength box is where your input into the process is required. Check the effect on the background and whether there is any detrimental adjustment to the foreground figures. If not, apply it.

6 If you're confused by the settings of any of these filters, clicking on the Help button will make it perfectly clear.

Unsharp Mask

One of the key tools in the digital photographer's armoury also has the strangest name

OUT OF FOCUS

If a picture is blurred then there is little you can do to it. USM won't work very well, but you can apply the Sharpen filter repeatedly, as long as you accept that the picture is going to look rougher and grainer by doing so. If the image is black and white you can get away with doing this to some extent.

Most digital cameras produce slightly soft photographs. If you're just snapping the family then this doesn't really matter, but if you want more polished results you should sharpen the picture on your PC. Traditional PC-based sharpening tools will improve an image and make it sharper, but they can also make pictures look grainier with pixelated elements that virtually ruin it.

The USM filter is different in that it doesn't actually sharpen the picture. Instead, it looks for boundaries between colours and tones, which it identifies as borders or textured features. It then lightens the light tones and darkens the dark tones, thus increasing the contrast between them. The result is edges and textures that stand out more, giving the impression that the

image is sharper. A secondary advantage of USM is that the picture also gets a contrast boost. Unfortunately, USM hits problems when land borders sky or objects border diffuse backgrounds – a noticeable halo effect can result.

There is nothing wrong with this picture, but as it came straight out of a digital camera it could benefit from a little sharpening

IN DETAIL UNSHARP MASK
Use the settings carefully to minimise the chances of a halo effect

1 There are a few useful Preset options that can be used for sharpening and changing the degree of application.

2 The original photo window. As you are sampling areas this can be panned around like the preview window.

3 This shows the effect of the USM filter. Check land and object edges for signs of haloes and if present, change the settings.

4 Having detected the edges, this setting tells the filter how many pixels surrounding the edge it should apply the effect to. Smaller values (0.5-1) are good for Web images, larger values (2-3) should be used for high-res print images.

5 This is the amount of contrast that will be applied to the selected pixels. A value of 50 will give a noticeable but subtle result, without causing haloes.

6 This value determines what the program considers to be a border or texture worth sharpening. It sets the difference in lightness value that adjacent pixels must have for the filter to be triggered.

7 Ticking this changes the luminance, so that the edges will be lighter or darker. It is a more subtle effect.

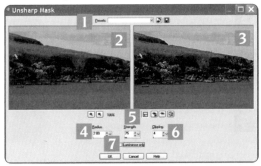

STEP BY STEP

USING UNSHARP MASK

1 With a Clipping value of 10, only distinct differences will be detected. Typically, most parts of the photo will not be enhanced, but the edge of an object or the edge of the landscape against the sky will be picked up. You don't want this because the edge of the land- scape is generally very visible, so you will get a distinct halo along the edge. The Strength value of 75 is only medium, so with this combination we get a result that isn't acceptable.

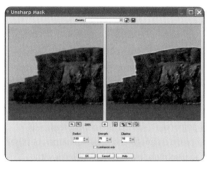

2 By reducing the Clipping to 4, much more of the landscape is detected and textures and shapes in rocks are brought out. While this makes the photo more impressive, the halo along the horizon is just as noticeable as before. One solution is to create a duplicate layer in the Layers palette, apply the USM filter to this and then set its Blend Mode to Darken. This prevents the white halo around the edge of objects, but speckles the picture with black dots.

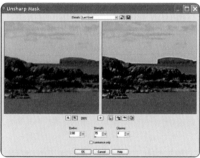

3 By now you can see that using the USM filter is a juggling act. However, consider this – the reason you sharpen a picture is to bring out more detail, to make it look punchier and sharper. You don't want to use it just to make the horizon is more obvious. Hence, our personal solution to this quandary is to use the Freehand selection tool to mark around all of the landscape, just short of the horizon and the landscape elements on it.

4 Feather the selection by about 30 pixels to give it a gradual decrease in effect that extends towards the horizon, without actually getting there. Apply the USM effect – you should be able to get away with a strength of 100. All the textures and features within the photo will become sharper, with more contrast, except for the horizon. However, as you can clearly see the horizon defined against the sky, this doesn't matter and you end up with a much better picture, without the halo effect.

EXTREME CORRECTION

The Sharpen command works by increasing the contrast between pixels, but does so in an automatic process applied to all pixels. This does sharpen the picture but can cause it to become pixelated very quickly. It is worth applying once if the picture only needs a very small tweak.

VIDEO TUTORIAL #14

 See this process being applied in the video tutorial, which shows how to sharpen while avoiding haloes around the edges of landscapes.

Distortion correction

If your images are bulging at the seams, you need to correct the distortion

HOW THE PROS DO IT

Ever wondered how glossy magazines manage to achieve house interior shots without a hint of distortion yet with a wide field of view? The answer is that the photographer uses specialist shift lenses on a medium- or large-format camera. The lens can be used to change the angle of light getting through to the film, thereby avoiding converging verticals and distortions.

The wider the lens you use, the greater the propensity for barrel distortion. The further you get from the centre, the more pronounced the effect becomes. This happens even with decent-quality lenses on an SLR, not just digital compact cameras that have smaller, inferior lenses. Paint Shop Pro 9 has three filters for tackling this problem.

The Barrel Distortion Correction filter is the most useful of these, followed by the Pincushion and Fisheye Distortion Correction filters (let's face it, you're unlikely to use a Fisheye lens by accident!). Only a very poor digital camera lens would produce a pincushion effect, but it does occur with compacts that boast an 8x or 10x zoom, as this pushes the optical quality of the device.

This is the kind of effect you get when photographing with a very wide-angle lens. The fisheye effect is even stranger and best suited to outdoor environments

IN DETAIL PINCUSHION CORRECTION

Using a massive optical zoom on a digital compact? Expect the pincushion effect

1 In the preview window you can see the results of using a 7x optical zoom on this picture. The column on the left bends towards the middle in a pincushion effect.

2 The Preset drop-down contains a number of different variations. You might, however, be better served making the alterations yourself.

3 Preview the effect in this window to see whether the original defect has been cured and to ensure that an additional one – barrel distortion – hasn't been created.

4 This is the control for the strength of the effect. As the bend on the pillar isn't that dramatic it only takes a setting of 5 to correct it.

5 Because the picture is being bent, white areas occur in places along the outside edge. Normally the program will automatically fill them in with cloned material, but if you tick this option it crops the picture to remove them instead.

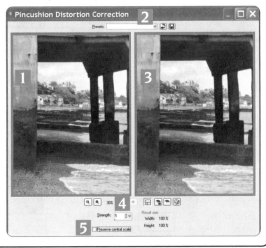

STEP BY STEP

BARREL DISTORTION CORRECTION

1 This picture has lots of barrel distortion along the top. Run the filter and go to the Presets. Here you'll find a number of interesting-sounding entries, but all they actually do is alter one variable. Enter a strength of 100 to see the effect. While the middle to lower portion of the picture is fine, and you can't see the bottom anyway, the top has been distorted in the other direction.

2 Enter a Strength of 40 and the result is far more acceptable. The bending horizontal line of the window at the top of the picture is much straighter. Unfortunately, the window strut to the right now bends in slightly. There are two things you could do to remedy this. The first is to mask it off with a feathered edge before applying the filter and then cloning the joins together. The second is to use the Clone tool to shave some of the slight bend off on the left-hand side.

3 An alternative is a filter under the Distortion list. This is called the Lens Distortion filter and it basically offers to perform the three kinds of action that the rest of the filters on this spread try to counter. However, it takes no great leap of intelligence to realise that the Pincushion setting can be used to counter a barrel distortion effect. The bonus of this filter is that you can position the centre point of the effect.

4 There are extra options available as well as the Strength, Position and Distortion type, though they are of more interest when you are using the Fisheye filter. Fisheye distortion is extreme, making the image bend like a bowl, so a decision has to be made regarding what fills the gaps. You can use the background colour, which is OK if your image is framed by that colour (like black) anyway. The other options are to either repeat the image edge or wrap it around.

OTHER OPTIONS

PSP 9 includes a number of geometric distortion filters from previous editions – it may be that these can do a better job. Look under Effects/ Distortion Effects to see what's available.

Red-eye removal

Aim and fire then count the cost of blood-red eyes. Here's some first aid

RED-EYE MODE

Reducing red-eye caused by a built-in flash is possible if you use a red-eye flash mode. This fires shards of light at the recipient's eyes, causing the pupils to contract, making it harder, but not impossible, for red-eye to occur.

The trouble with the on-camera flash is that it is positioned too close to the lens so that it travels directly along the path towards the subject that also leads back to the camera. When the flash hits the eye, it enters the retina and illuminates the blood vessels at the back of the cornea. As the return angle for the light is right back to the camera, hey presto – red-eye. Although most digital cameras have a red-eye reduction mode, the only way to completely avoid red-eye is to use an external flash gun mounted away from the lens. The return path is then completely different and the effect doesn't occur. Alternatively, with a flexible flash gun unit you can bounce light off surfaces like walls to create a very diffuse light, meaning there's no chance of red-eye.

PSP 9's clever filter makes correcting red-eye easy. The process consists of creating an iris shape, placing it over the subject's eye and then tweaking the settings so that it blends in with the original.

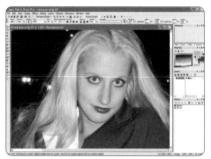

Achieve great results with this clever tool

IN DETAIL RED-EYE REMOVAL

Stop your subjects looking like the undead on a night out

1 This is the source window and it's here that you draw a circle to define the iris. You can then move it over the subject's eye and resize it to fit.

2 The result of the process shows up here, so if it doesn't look right then keep at it as excellent results are possible.

3 There are different Method options available for humans and animals.

4 These tweak the settings that determine how the eye is treated and how the catchlight, or glint, will appear.

5 Use this to set the colour of the subject's eyes. Unfortunately, the choice of colours is slightly limited.

6 Feather and Blur control how the new iris is blended over the old one.

7 Select the shade of the colour chosen in step 5. These tend to be quite dark, though there are a couple of light shades.

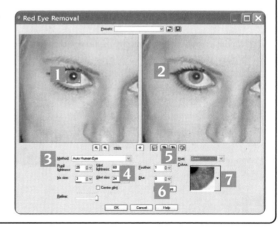

Hue & Saturation

Make your colours come alive with these straightforward controls

Digital cameras can produce colours that are weak or of limited range. Most digital cameras use a colour space called sRGB, which has a limited range (referred to as a gamut) but is suitable for images that are to be used on the Web or passed between devices. However, many recent models offer the much wider gamut of Adobe RGB. The tones produced by sRGB colour space can look flat. That's where the Hue/Saturation/Lightness filter comes in as it allows individual colour elements to be manipulated, as well as changed to new colours entirely.

You can select and alter individual colour components. This is very useful because a general saturation increase can lead to the appearance of digital artefacts or noise. If your image has a colour cast, or uses a colour you don't like in the background, this can be selected and the hue shifted to a more favourable colour. This usually entails masking off areas of the image as every incidence of the colour and its variants on the colour wheel will be shifted.

Poor colour saturation is remedied here with a targeted red and yellow saturation enhancement

CAMERA SETTINGS

If your camera has a choice of RGB colour spaces, choose Adobe RGB 1998 as it has a much wider range of colours.

IN DETAIL **HUE & SATURATION**
Use these tools to improve the colours in your image

1 The list of Presets offers a couple of interesting special effects that can be applied using this filter.

2 The preview window shows the colour changes. If you are targeting specific colours, it's worth clicking on the proof icon to see how it all works together.

3 The various colour components can be individually selected or the entire range manipulated from here.

4 The Hue is the actual colour value. Shifting it changes it to a different colour altogether. If an individual colour has been selected, the colour wheel will show where it is and what colours border it. The wheel or the Hue setting can be used to change them.

5 The Saturation is the amount of the hue present. It sets how pallid or garish your image is.

6 The Lightness option simply makes the colour lighter or darker.

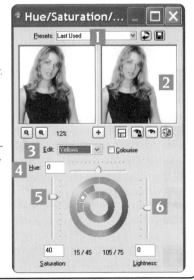

Levels and Curves

Enhance the tonal range of your image and make it come to life

LATITUDE
This refers to the camera's ability to capture a wide range of tones. Print film has a wide latitude, which means that even if you get the exposure wrong you'll still get a good result. Digital has a much narrower latitude, so if you get the exposure wrong the picture may be over-exposed and will lose the highlight detail.

Digital camera images tend to be flat and lack contrast. They can also be underexposed, not because the metering system has been fooled, but because the current generation of digital cameras have limited exposure latitude. As a result, the camera prevents detail being lost in the highlights by slightly underexposing.

The Levels and Curves tools are designed to give your underexposed, drab photos a boost. They both do a similar thing, just in different ways. Levels has a Stretch Histogram feature (similar to that in Photoshop) that extends the tonal range of the image so that it uses the full range available. The tool also allows you to control where the mid-tones occur and how light or dark the shadows and

highlights are. Curves is slightly different in that it allows you to actively manipulate the shadows, mid-tones and highlights, often without disturbing the other components.

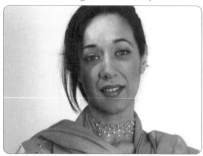

This is an original image straight from the digital camera. Note that the background is a grubby white and the picture lacks contrast

IN DETAIL LEVELS

Use the Levels tool to enhance tonal range and shift the mid-tone point

1 The Preset box not only contains settings that brighten images, but individual channel settings that create special effects.

2 The source window shows the original, flat digital image.

3 In the preview window you can see the difference the settings are making.

4 You can either manipulate individual colour channels or all of them at once.

5 The Input Levels show the range of bright tones used

in the image. If you move the black carat on the left, towards the right, the image will get darker. If you move the right-hand white carat to the left, all the tones to the right of it will turn white.

6 The Output Levels shows the tones the image will use when you click OK. If you move the left-hand black carat to the right, fewer black tones will be used and the image will lighten. Move the white carat on the right, to the left and the image will use fewer white tones, becoming darker.

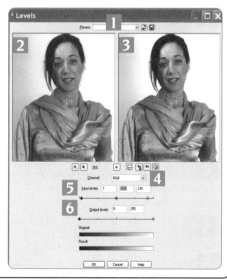

STEP BY STEP

USING CURVES

1 Here, the aperture priority zone metering has been influenced by the brightness of the sky and has underexposed the photo. The Histogram shows that the main data in terms of luminance, which sets the contrast, is in the left third of the display. There is some data the rest of the way along, which in the image is the clouds and the white rocks. When using Levels to enhance an image like this, it would be easy to lose detail from these highlights.

2 Run the Curves dialog. On the box shown, the Input runs along the top and Output runs down the left. This means the two are combined so that you can manipulate the data. The mid-tones of the image are based around the centre of the diagonal line that runs from bottom left (the dark shades) to top right (the light shades). By clicking on the line you create control points that can then be used to manipulate the line and hence the tonal data.

3 Add three control points and create an exaggerated curve. To remove a control point, grab it and drag it off screen. Add one in the centre to control the mid-tones, one halfway up the line for the highlights and one halfway down the line for the shadows. If you only added one point, dragging it up to the left or down to the right would unbalance the Input and Output values. If the Input is more than the Output the image will darken and vice versa.

4 As you can see, this has given the image too strong a contrast and too many dark elements. As the image needs brightening as well as contrast enhancement, move the top control point up to the left and the bottom point down to the right by modest amounts. Grab the central point and move it up to the left a little. This will brighten the mid-tones and the shadows and highlights will gain more contrast through the other manipulations. Click OK to apply these changes to the image.

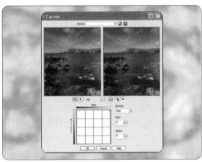

VIDEO TUTORIAL #15

Watch the video tutorial to learn how to use Levels and Curves to increase contrast and give the image more punch.

ON THE CD

Both images from the tutorial are on the CD in low-resolution form. Use them to have a go at using Levels and Curves.

Blur tools

Diffuse backgrounds or add motion effects with the Blur tool

TELEPHOTO BURST

There's a trick in regular photography involving a zoom lens. As the fire button is pressed (there's usually a fairly slow shutter speed) the zoom is extended, creating a picture with a zoom burst effect. This can be duplicated with the Radial Blur filter.

Diffusing the background is a recognised shooting technique for portraits, as it focuses attention on the subject. To achieve a diffuse background, shoot using a wide aperture. However, there's a problem that is unique to digital compact cameras. Because the CCD is very small it generates greater depth of field than the aperture setting indicates – up to four or five times as much. So, when you set the aperture to f2.8, the depth of field is more like that you would get from f11 or f16. Hardly conducive to achieving diffuse backgrounds or good portraits.

The Blur options in Paint Shop Pro consist of regular Blur and stronger versions – Radial Blur, Motion Blur and Gaussian Blur. Radial Blur whirls the picture around as if it were going down a plughole, but without the distortion that entails, just the blur. Motion Blur can be used to make something look like it's moving. Gaussian Blur is the standard blur tool – we look at this in the step-by-step opposite.

By masking the front grill and applying a motion blur this Buick Century is given a sense of movement

IN DETAIL RADIAL BLUR
Apply a number of dramatic effects, not just radial

1 Set the centre of the effect in the source window.

2 The preview window shows the effect in action, and recalculates it every time you resize the dialog box.

3 There are three types of effect. The Spin whips things round in a circular fashion. The Zoom gives the effect seen here. The Twirl uses two spin cycles in opposite directions.

4 The Strength determines the level of the effect.

5 If the picture is a portrait with a figure in it, you may want to tick this box so that it works on an elliptical basis rather than circular.

6 The offsets can be used to accurately position the effect centrally, but really, it's easier to do it by hand.

7 This figure sets how much of the centre of the image is protected from the radial effect. When used with the Zoom effect it enables you to leave a point of focus.

STEP BY STEP

GAUSSIAN BLUR

1 This is a typical picture of someone in their front room. It was taken with an Olympus digital SLR, at an f2 aperture. However, this particular camera used a small format CCD, so that the f2 aperture, which should have left the background totally out of focus, has had the effect of f8-f11. While the background isn't sharp, it's still visible enough to see that wooden plank rising out of the back of the subject's head.

2 The first task, then, is to select around the figure. The fact that it's just a head shot makes life easier as there are only two depths to the picture – the foreground with the subject in it and the background that needs diffusing. So, using the Freehand Selection tool, with the Point to Point option, zoom in to 200% and select around the girl.

3 Hold down the Control key to remove bits through the hair from the selection – selecting hair is a project dealt with in an upcoming issue. Go to Selections/ Modify/ Feather and enter a value of 2 pixels to soften the edge. Then go to Selection and Modify again but this time choose the Contract option. Enter a value of 1 pixel to pull the selection back to make it really tight.

4 The quick and easy method now is to invert the selection and then run the Gaussian Blur filter. This can lead to a halo effect around the figure as the filter picks up bits from beyond the edge of the feathering selection when calculating the blur. There is a way around this, which will be dealt with in a project in two issues' time. For now, apply a Gaussian Blur of 10 pixels to blur the background and make the foreground figure stand out.

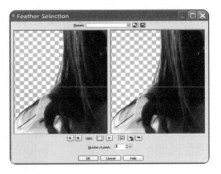

ON THE CD
The picture used in this tutorial is on the CD so you can have a go at selecting the figure and blurring the background.

Artefact removal

The JPEG system is marvellous for squeezing large images into a small space, but at a price...

DEGRADING
Unless you specifically need to save space, whether on a memory card or webpage, avoid using JPEGs, as constant resaving will degrade the image quality each time.

While they're always the first choice, TIFFs occupy a lot of space. JPEGs are much more space friendly, but if you're going to use them, put the quality setting onto its highest level. Some cameras use 100% quality, lossless compression, but others will always lose some quality along the way.

The JPEG system works by describing blocks of image data, rather than representing individual pixels. This is fine in wide-open areas of the same colour, but it struggles when the scene has a splash of different tones and textures. Where two join, such as buildings sticking into the sky, compression artefacts will invariably run down the side. Paint Shop Pro's JPEG Artifact Removal filter is designed to smooth these out, but by doing so it starts to soften

the image, making it something of a balancing act. Once you've used the filter on an image, don't save it as a JPEG again.

In this heavily compressed picture, artefacts have appeared in the trees and next to the steeple

IN DETAIL JPEG ARTIFACT REMOVAL FILTER
Use the filter to clean out boxy-looking artefacts

1 The original image shows distinctive box-like JPEG artefacts along the steeple. The sky has been ruined as well.

2 The preview window shows how effective the removal is and, importantly, how soft the image will be as a result.

3 There are some Presets, but we recommend you work through the options yourself to get the best results.

4 It's worth zooming right in so you can get a good idea of the effect of the processing.

5 The Strength setting determines how well the artefacts are dealt with and how soft the resulting picture will be.

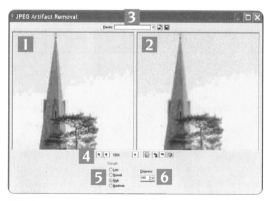

6 The more Strength you use, the more Crispness you'll need to apply. This is a sharpening routine that restores some detail to the image. It generates a lot of digital noise at 100%

Edge preserving

Pictures looking a bit grainy? Smooth them without losing the edges

Film grain is a beautiful thing and can make a mono image. But should you wish to avoid it, there are high ISO colour films that exhibit very little grain. That's not the case in the digital world, however. You shoot at high ISOs because there's little light and flash would ruin the atmosphere. The result will depend on the camera, but at ISO 800 digital noise will certainly occur. This isn't so bad on black and white images, but it will ruin colour pictures.

There are a couple of Paint Shop Pro filters designed to tackle this, beyond the one specifically for digital noise (see page 62). The Edge Preserving Smooth filter is designed to look for and preserve edges, and smooth out the contents. This retains the structure of the photo but removes the unpleasantness. It's best suited to use with portraits as a loss of detail is inherent to the process. Try converting landscape photos that suffer from a lot of noise to monochrome, rather than torturing them with this filter.

Here, a Smoothing factor of 22 preserved outlines and shape, while the interior contents became more like paint dabs than grain

DIGITAL ISO
The higher the digital ISO you use on a camera, the more likely digital noise is to occur. Once you get above ISO 400 you can expect lots of noise, particularly on smaller, compact cameras.

TEXTURE PRESERVING SMOOTH
Want to smooth out some parts of your picture but preserve the textures?

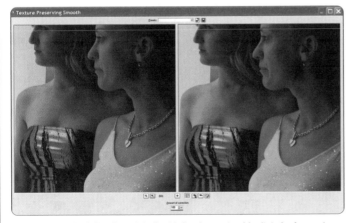

The picture on the left is the original, with fine but noticeable digital colour noise. In the preview on the right, the filter has blended in the noise to make it much more subtle on the skin tones, but preserved the textures and colours of the outfits

While it might sound like a contradiction in terms, the Texture Preserving Smooth filter is designed to preserve texture details while removing digital noise or specks from scanned film. It works by assessing the pixels, together with their neighbours, so that batches that have obvious textures are left untouched, while those that look like normal, smooth areas, but with lots of noise are smoothed out. It should mean that things like faces and skin tones are smoothed but clothes remain textured, so it's good for portraits. Go to Adjust/ Add/Remove Noise/ Texture Preserving Smooth to run it.

LESSON 4
Photo correction
Enhance and smarten up this photo of an Oystercatcher

WHAT WILL YOU LEARN?
- **Sharpen really soft pictures**
- **Remove noise**
- **Fix overexposure**
- **Enhance separate colours**
- **Use Curves selectively**

SHOOTING BIRDS

Photographing birds in flight is notoriously difficult for two reasons – not only is it hard to focus on the bird as it wheels around the sky, but you need a fast enough shutter speed when using a zoom. Aside from getting as close as possible, the best advice we can give is to watch the patterns of the bird and try to shoot it when it banks or turns into the wind as it will be moving at its slowest.

STEP BY STEP

1 Professionals use big zooms with a wide maximum aperture, which cost £3,000+. Hobbyists therefore make do with a shorter zoom and a slower aperture. This results in camera shake and lack of contrast, as seen here. The picture is overexposed, soft, and lacking in colour.

2 Go to the Levels command. As the picture is overexposed, all the blacks are a muddy grey. Grab hold of the black carat on the left of the Input Level bar and move it to the right until it registers 28 in the Input Level box. As you do this the mid-tone carat will shuffle along to the right. This will lighten the mid-tones even more which we don't want, so grab hold of it and drag it back to the middle.

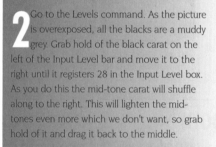

3 There is nothing going on in the upper right-hand side of the picture and although the bird is soaring, its body is in the lower half of the picture. Select the Crop tool and draw a box around the bird. Use the handles at the mid-points of each side to resize it. Grab near the middle to move the entire crop square about. Use the crop to create a tighter composition. Press the tick to apply.

4 Now the bird is quite soft. Rather than use the Unsharp Mask filter at its defaults to tackle this, we can take it further. The Radius sets how many pixels will be brightened at the edges. If this figure is much higher, there won't be a halo as such, just a lot of high contrast elements, which is too strong for some parts of the photo. To rectify this, right-click on the Background layer and select Duplicate layer.

STEP BY STEP

5 Select the Duplicate layer, then go to the Unsharp Mask filter. Enter 15 for the Radius, 100 for Strength and 4 for Clipping. This will make the bird stand out but will overexpose parts of it. Reduce the Opacity of the duplicate layer to 50%, which will stop it being so horribly contrasty. Select the Eraser and set the Opacity to 20%, then rub at the overexposed rear feathers, the part just behind the black feathers on the head, and around the eye so it's visible.

6 Go to Layers/ Merge/ Merge All (Flatten) to flatten and incorporate the edited layer. Next, go to Adjust and select Sharpen then Sharpen More. This will really make it stand out, but will introduce noise and grain. So, the next filter to run is Edge Preserving Smooth. Go to Enhance Photo and select it from there. Enter a Strength of 3, which will fade the noise enough but won't affect the sharper edge we've created.

7 While there aren't many colours in this image, the beak should be more like the orange of a carrot. Go to Adjust/ Hue and Saturation/ Hue/Saturation/Lightness. In the Edit box, select Reds then enter a Saturation value of 30. Next, select the Cyans and enter a Saturation value of 10. This will give a slight tinge to the background – any more creates a better effect but generates lots of noise.

8 Finally, run the Curves adjustment. Click on the middle of the curve line to hold the mid-tones. Add a control point halfway between the bottom and the next point. Move this down and right to darken the dark tones. Click on the bird's head in the actual picture to add a control point based on the brightness of the head. Move this point back up so it is in a straight corner-to-corner line. Click on the bird's plumage in the picture to generate another point and move this up and left. Click OK to finish.

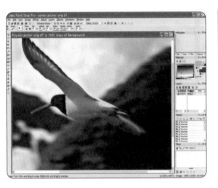

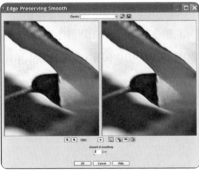

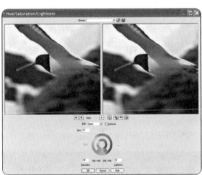

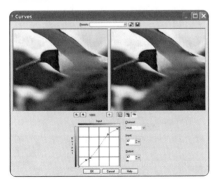

VIDEO TUTORIAL #16

See this detailed photo adjustment in action in the video tutorial provided. You could even have a go yourself...

ON THE CD

A copy of the Oystercatcher picture is provided on the CD. See how good a job you can make of improving this slightly out of focus bird.

CHAPTER 5
All about layers

Often the most misunderstood or confusing aspect of digital editing, layers are actually your most useful ally. In this chapter we'll show you how to take full advantage of the fantastic possibilities they present

L ayers can be difficult to get to grips with if you are a newcomer to digital editing. The whole concept is rather baffling, but it needn't be. Layers can be your best friend in digital manipulation, allowing you not only to create complex images, but also to carry out skilful enhancements that give a natural finish. Part of the confusion comes when anyone who has used Photoshop moves over to Paint Shop Pro, because while PSP layers are Photoshop-compatible and vice versa, there are some important differences.

To help make sense of layers, think of them this way. Take a photographic print – that's your background, your base layer. Now place anoth-er print on top of it. Now you can't see the bottom print, but it's still there. However, we can change the characteristics of this top print, for instance by reducing its opacity (making it transparent). The degree of opacity can be any-thing from 1% to 99%. At 100% the layer is totally solid and you can't see through it. At any other setting, it's as if we'd placed a photo-graphic slide over the background print, rather than another print. You can see both the top image, and something of the one underneath.

You can also set how the pixels in that top layer react with those underneath. This is called the Blend Mode, and there are quite a few of these available. They compare pixels on each

DISCOVER IN THIS CHAPTER →

How to combine Raster layers to give your drab photos an instant contrast boost.

How to use Art Media layers to create paintings or turn your photos into one.

layer directly: some, for example, multiply the contents so that the resulting composite has more contrast.

The key point to realise is that layers work from the bottom upwards. The Background layer doesn't combine with anything because it's on the bottom. A layer above it in the Layers palette combines with the Background layer, depending on the Blend Mode and Opacity settings. The result of this is what you see on screen. If there is another layer above this, that combines with the result of the two layers below. If there is another layer above this, it combines with the result of the second layer, combining with the result of the first

layer plus the background layer. It can be confusing, but just work your way up, and add the results as you go.

Layers can also be turned on or off. At times you might want to do this just to see the result of different combinations. This can also help when you are applying certain effects.

There are three main types of layers – Raster, Art Media and Vector. Raster layers deal with photographs or pixel-based images; Art Media layers are the new boys to PSP 9 and allow art materials to be used; and Vector layers are used for text and objects created from points. There are also Adjustment layers to consider, but more on those further on.

WELL ADJUSTED
The picture of Dunkeld bridge in Perth & Kinross has been manipulated with an Adjustment layer to restore the late evening sunlight that was present at the scene.

The Adjustment layer comes with a built-in mask to enable you to apply effects selectively.

Follow the project to replace the useless sky in this seascape with one that is more engaging.

VIDEO TUTORIAL

The video tutorial at the end of the chapter shows how the replacement sky image was created.

Raster layers

The most common layer type in PSP is ideal for manipulating your digital images

COMPATIBILITY
Raster layers in PSP are perfectly compatible with Photoshop, so images composed solely of them can be saved in the .psd format without risk.

It may sound scary, but a Raster layer is simply one which consists of a series of pixels that make up an image, all with the potential for separate colour values. A Raster layer can therefore contain photographs or pictures, but not vector objects, or the Art Materials introduced with Paint Shop Pro 9 – these have their own layer types.

The great thing about layers is that you can combine them, or parts of them, or create effects by using the layer blending options.

When you have finished creating your artwork

or editing a picture, you should flatten the layers – firstly because many file formats don't support multiple layers, and secondly because you don't want to show everyone how your image was constructed. However, you should always retain a copy of the picture with all the layers intact, so that you can edit the project later if required. It's best to use the .psp file format for this, because whilst other multi-layer formats (including Photoshop's .psd format) are compatible with Raster layers, they do not support all of PSP's other layer types.

BLENDING IN ACTION
Use the blending layers to create specific effects

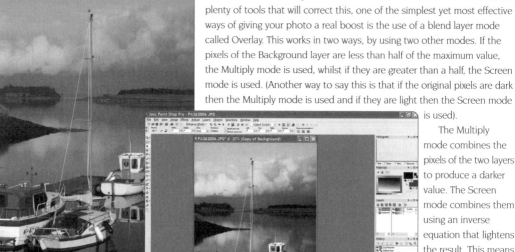

It's often the case that pictures are flat and lack contrast. While there are plenty of tools that will correct this, one of the simplest yet most effective ways of giving your photo a real boost is the use of a blend layer mode called Overlay. This works in two ways, by using two other modes. If the pixels of the Background layer are less than half of the maximum value, the Multiply mode is used, whilst if they are greater than a half, the Screen mode is used. (Another way to say this is that if the original pixels are dark then the Multiply mode is used and if they are light then the Screen mode is used).

The Multiply mode combines the pixels of the two layers to produce a darker value. The Screen mode combines them using an inverse equation that lightens the result. This means that the overall effect of the Overlay blend mode is to stretch the tonal range, giving the picture more contrast.

The original image is very nice, but it is flat with subdued colours

The image was loaded into PSP, a duplicate layer created and the Blend Mode set to Overlay. The picture gets an instant boost

Vector layers

These layers are designed to hold scalable objects and text

Whereas a Raster layer is composed of information about individual pixels, a Vector layer contains information about points and the lines between them. This means Vector layers can initially be harder to get to grips with than Raster layers, but they are a lot more flexible and can be used to create intricate illustrations. Objects on Vector layers can be resized, recoloured and moved around at will. They can have extra parts added and be deformed and manipulated into entirely new shapes.

Text is also counted as a vector object, and appears on a Vector layer. This means that it can be manipulated, distorted, rotated and resized as desired, with no loss of quality.

You can apply a number of filters and effects to a Vector layer, but some can only be applied to Raster layers, so that if you try to apply them to the layer it will ask if you'd like to convert the layer into a Raster. If you do this, remember that you will lose the editing flexibility that was available when it was a Vector layer.

Create graphic shapes and incorporate text in the Vector layer system

PAINT ON VECTORS
If you attempt to draw or paint on a Vector layer, Paint Shop Pro will tell you that the layer must be converted to a Raster to proceed. If you do this, all your objects and text will be turned into graphics.

IN DETAIL VECTOR LAYER
See how the image above breaks down as a Vector layer

1 Unlike Raster layers, Vector layers break down into groups depending on how they were created. The pram and text fall under one grouping.

2 The grouping has its own Opacity and Blend Mode.

3 A mask can be applied to the overall grouping, to hide or show parts as desired.

4 Within the overall group, this is the vector cluster that forms all the objects on the screen. The text could have been a different vector cluster within the grouping.

5 Each separate vector cluster of objects has its own opacity and Blend Mode.

6 These are the individual elements that go to make up Vector 1 – starting with the text element.

7 Here are the parts of the path that made the pram. We've grouped them all together is so that they make one entire object which can then be assigned an overall Opacity and Blend Mode, rather than having to set Opacity/Blend Modes for every little part.

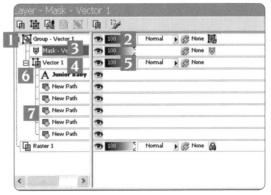

Art Media layers

Meet the new feature that takes the painting element of Paint Shop Pro to the next level

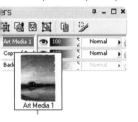

There's little doubt that the painting features of Paint Shop Pro have in the past been one of the weakest parts of the program. Without the ability to create even the illusion of depth to the paint, the existing tools looked false. Only the charcoal or pencil effects were even worth bothering with. However, that has all changed with the advent of the Art Media layer, which is there for you to paint the artist materials on.

The Art Media layer can be set to be a dry paint or a wet paint layer, which affects how items on the layer combine and react. There's no great science here as this isn't a rival to Corel Painter, but it does make a difference and it's worth setting this before you start painting.

Perhaps the most exciting feature of this layer is the Trace function. This works by allowing whatever brush is being used to pick up the colours of a Raster layer underneath the Art Media layer. This means you can create a painting based on your photograph. Alternatively you can just paint or sketch from scratch.

A simple photo forms the basis for an interesting effect. Using an Art Media layer with the Trace option turned on, a large oil paint brush was used to pick up the colour from the photo beneath

TEXTURE BACKGROUNDS
Add an artistic finish to your efforts

You can select a canvas texture to apply to an Art Media layer. There are a wide range of artistic canvas backgrounds available – fine and coarse effects, on various paper types. However, since Art Media layers are empty when first created, the effects of the textured background you've selected don't become apparent until you start splashing paint on top of them.

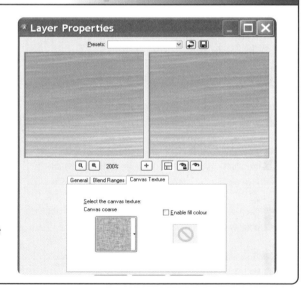

This dialog allows you to select a canvas effect to work with the Art Media layer

Blending modes

The Blend Mode sets how a layer is combined with the one underneath

Without the blending modes, the layers system would be useful, but not capable of the great variety of effects and uses that it can be put to. Therefore, understanding blending modes is key to being able use them to enhance your images. Here are the types, minus the ones marked Legacy, as they are simply versions from previous releases of PSP and are only included for compatibility.

EXPERIMENT
The best way to get a feel for blending modes is to duplicate an image and then try out each mode in turn to see what it does.

Darken – Where pixels in the top layer are darker than those underneath, they are displayed. If they are not darker, then the pixels from the layer underneath are displayed instead.

Lighten – The opposite of the above layer. Where pixels are lighter than those underneath, they are displayed. Otherwise, the pixels from the layer underneath are displayed instead.

Hue – The Hue is the absolute colour, minus saturation or lightness values. The blend mode applies the hue of the colours of the top image, over the ones of the bottom.

Saturation – This is the amount of colour in a pixel in the top layer. It is applied to the layer below, regardless of whether it is strong or weak. It changes the saturation level of the layer below, to that of the overlying layer.

Colour – Similar to the Hue blend mode, this applies both hue and saturation from the top layer to the bottom layer.

Luminance – This is the lightness, or the tonality of the image. The luminance of the top layer is applied to the bottom layer, without affecting hue and saturation. As Luminance is effectively what defines the shape of the contents of the layer, it means that whatever is in the top layer will form the object, but the hue and saturation will be from the bottom layer.

Multiply – This multiplies the colours of the two layers together, producing a darker image, but often one with considerably more contrast.

Screen – The opposite of the above layer. It multiplies the values, then inverts them so that the picture becomes lighter overall.

Dissolve – A bit of a gimmicky effect. The top layer is randomly blended into the bottom layer, with the amount of blending set by the opacity of the top layer. The more opaque it is, the more the pixels of the layer below will be promoted to full strength in the result.

Overlay – One of the clever modes. If the colour of the bottom layer's pixels are dark (ie less than half of the maximum value), they are multiplied with the top layer. If the pixels are lighter, then they are multiplied and the inverse result used.

Hard Light – This works like the above layer, except that the calculations are carried out on the uppermost layer.

Dodge – This lightens the result by using the lightness values of the top layer to lighten those of the layer underneath. The result is the image in the bottom layer, but with lighter pixels.

Burn – The opposite of Dodge – it reduces the lightness values.

Soft Light – A combo mode. If the colour value of the top layer pixels are less than half (ie darker) then the Burn blend mode is applied, otherwise the Dodge mode is applied. This makes parts of images lighter and darker but in a more subtle fashion that the Overlay mode.

Difference and Exclusion – Both of these blend modes subtract the colour values of the top layer from those of the bottom. The Exclusion mode is more subtle than the Different mode.

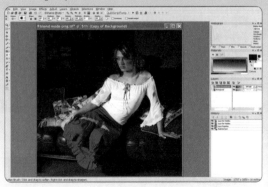

A duplicate layer of this image was created and the Blend Mode set to Soft Light. This added highlights and shadows, making the image have a more dynamic contrast

Adjustment layers

If an image doesn't quite work then you need to make adjustments

ALTERNATIVES

If the effect you want to apply isn't on the Adjustment layer list then you will have to create a Mask layer, with the source as the image.

An Adjustment layer doesn't have pixel or vector contents. Instead, it simply performs an action on the layer below. Adjustment layers have a built-in mask ability. Select the Paintbrush and black paint and you can paint on the Adjustment layer. This masks off the effect from that part of the image, allowing you to target where the effect is applied. If you make a mistake, swap to white and paint over the mask again to restore the effect to that part of the image. You can even vary the opacity of the brush to vary the application of the effect throughout the image.

There might be dark areas of the image where you can't see whether you've painted on the mask or not. Helpfully, there's an option to display the mask as a red, transparent effect

so you can see where it is being applied – where you can see red, the adjustment works to full effect, and where there is no red, the effect is blocked.

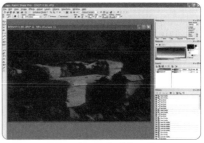

Here you can see the mask of the Adjustment layer. In the reddest bits the effect will be at its fullest – it will be blocked where there is no red

ADJUSTMENT EFFECTS
So what are the standard range of adjustments?

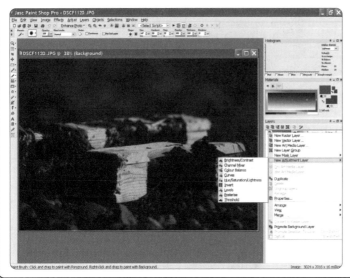

What can you do with your adjustments then? This is actually a very important question, because it dictates what you can easily use with an Adjustment layer, and what can only be achieved by using a Layer mask and a duplicate of the image. All the obvious options are available, including Brightness/Contrast, Curves, Levels, and Hue/Saturation/Lightness. There are also some less obvious but no less interesting ones, such as Channel Mixer, Colour Balance, Invert, Posterise and Threshold.

Right-click on a layer and choose the adjustments you want to apply

USING ADJUSTMENT LAYERS

1 This picture was shot with a digital SLR late in the afternoon. The sky was a deep blue, but you wouldn't know it from the dreary colours that the camera produced. Part of the problem was that the White Balance of the camera was left on Automatic, so it saw the lovely yellow-orange glow as a potential colour cast, and adjusted the picture automatically. As a result, instead of golden stonework, we have a drab bridge.

2 Right-click on the Background layer and select New Adjustment Layer. Select the Hue/Saturation/Lightness option. You would normally have to pick colour channels to enhance, but with an Adjustment layer, you can pick out the region of the picture you are going to apply the full adjustment to, and use that to judge how much to apply. We looked at the bridge and adjusted until it looked right. Other parts of the picture look putrid but don't worry about that.

3 Select a large paintbrush and set the Opacity to 25%. In the Materials palette, ensure that the foreground colour is pure black and the background is pure white. You can only choose from a range of black to white because the mask is greyscale. (It doesn't need colour because it is simply setting the opacity for individual pixels.) Brush through the sky and background hills, as they are a little overdone and noise is appearing.

4 Paint the mask over the grass and the river. Change to a smaller brush and paint over the grass again, reducing the saturation effect by a combined 50%. Click on the Mask Overlay Toggle icon in the Layer palette to see the red overlay. Toggle it off again and paint anywhere that obvious discrepancies were seen on the red overlay. If you need to erase the mask, simply swap foreground and background colours around – white will remove it. Flatten the layers and save the end result.

VIDEO TUTORIAL #17

See how to apply the layer and paint on the mask to moderate the effect.

ON THE CD
There is a copy of the image used here so that you can try out the Adjustment Layer tutorial yourself.

LESSON 5
Replacing skies

Use layer modes to replace a dull sky and give a hint of colour in the water

STEP BY STEP

1 The original image on the left shows some promise, but there are some problems. The sky is a deathly drab grey, the picture is slightly askew, and the colours and contrast are flat. The first thing to do is load the picture and the replacement sky picture (on the right).

2 In the sky picture, use the rectangular Selection tool to mark off a suitable area. Make this larger than you need to give you flexibility. Go to Edit/ Copy, switch to the main picture and select Edit/ Paste/ Paste As New Layer. Grab hold of the pasted sky and move it to the top of the screen, ensuring it covers the original sky. Rename this the sky layer. Click the Mask Show All icon in the Layers Palette.

3 Change the Blend Mode of the Group master layer to Colour. Select a black brush at 50% Opacity. Click on the Mask layer, then use the brush to paint over parts of the picture where you do not want the colour effect to apply. You will need two paint coverings to completely mask it off. It's worth leaving a little hint of light along the edge of the rock where it faces into the sky.

4 In the Layers palette, look to the Mask layer and click on the Mask Overlay Toggle. This shows a red glaze over the screen that represents the mask, enabling you to check it more easily. When you're satisfied with it, go to Layers and select Merge/ Merge All. Go back to your sky image and select an area that is only sky. Copy it, then Paste As New Layer again. This time go to Image and select Flip to turn it over.

STEP BY STEP

5 Move the layer so that it borders right against, and overlaps if necessary, the top of the sea and the start of the land. Reduce the layer Opacity to 60% so you can see through it. Then select the Deform Tool and pick the Scale option. Now drag and scale the sky layer so that it fits all the way across the image and all the way down to where the sea ends. Apply this then change the Opacity to 30% and change the Blend Mode to Colour. This should give a realistic watery look.

6 In the Layers palette, with the new watery layer selected, click on the Mask Show All icon. Select a black brush and set the Opacity to 15%. Paint out areas on the mask where there shouldn't be watery reflections. Where this layer overlaps the land, you should switch to 80% Opacity to remove it. Also use this setting to wipe over the boulders that have the watery layer over them. You'll be surprised to see colours suddenly come back up because you can't detect what the watery layer is doing.

7 Once these adjustments are completed, go to Layers/ Merge/ Merge All to flatten. Click on the Freehand Selection tool and choose the Point To Point type. Mark out an area to include all the land and sea, stopping short of the edge of the rocks on the left and the far land on the horizon. Feather the selection by 20 pixels. Now run Unsharp Mask and enter values of: Radius 2; Strength 100; Clipping 4. Apply it then deselect the selection by pressing Control+D.

8 Go to Adjust/ Hue And Saturation/ Hue/Saturation/Lightness. Increase the Saturation by 20%. Click on the background layer and select New Adjustment Layer. Pick the Curves adjustment and enter an S-shaped curve with three points. If there are areas on the photo that are too dark, or some highlights have been lost, use a black paintbrush at 20% Opacity to block the effect. Merge the layers when finished. Finally, if the sky has pixellated use the Soften brush to smooth it out, then save.

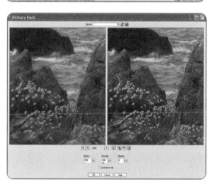

VIDEO TUTORIAL #18

Watch the various layers of this project being put together, then have a go yourself.

CHAPTER 6

Using text to better effect

Text can be incorporated into many images to create greeting cards, posters, promotional material, presentations and much more

YOU'LL DISCOVER HOW TO...

- Create text and place it in the image
- Use text as a selection
- Place text on a curve

Paint Shop Pro now offers a powerful and flexible text-creation system. However, it can be a little confusing when you first use it. For a start there are three types of text, provided via a tiny little box that is very easy to miss. The Create As drop-down list allows you to choose between creating text as a vector, a raster or as a selection.

Vector text

This is the most commonly chosen option. It can be created on any layer type. If the current layer is a Vector it will appear there; if it's any other type of layer, a Vector layer will be automatically created for it. As it's a vector, once the text is created you can go back and change the font, size, style, colour, alignment and spacing. You can also drag and resize it without any loss of quality. Best of all, you can actually change the wording so that if you make a spelling mistake it can be corrected after you've created it. What you can't do is apply paintbrush effects or some of the filters and tools that are specific to Raster images. If you try, PSP will ask if it's OK to change to a Raster layer to do so.

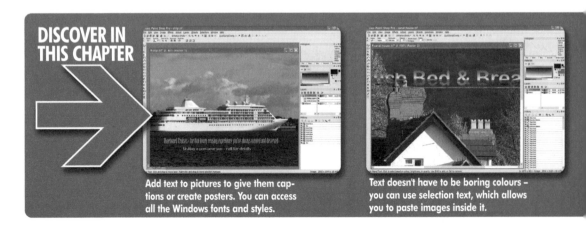

DISCOVER IN THIS CHAPTER

Add text to pictures to give them captions or create posters. You can access all the Windows fonts and styles.

Text doesn't have to be boring colours – you can use selection text, which allows you to paste images inside it.

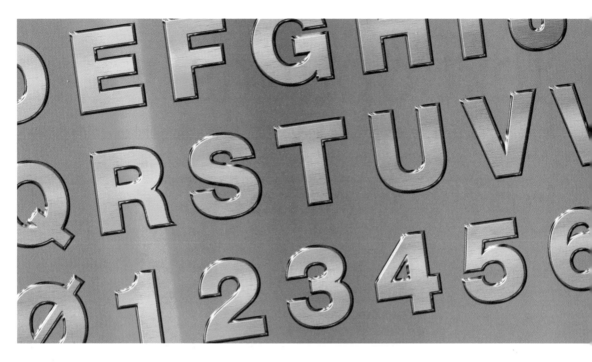

Raster text

If you create raster text when you are working on a Vector layer, PSP will automatically create a Raster layer for the text to go on. The text can use any of the usual qualities and components, but once it is applied it can no longer be edited as it becomes part of the background. It can be deformed and stretched, though each application of this will degrade the quality, unlike on a Vector layer. The advantage of creating raster text is that the whole range of filters is available to apply to it – just make sure you get the spelling and size right in the first place.

Text as a selection

The alternative to these is text as a selection. Once again, all the text formats and fonts are available, but when the text is applied it becomes a selection. This can be feathered or modified like any other selection. Perhaps the greatest advantage of text as a selection is that it allows you to paste other images inside the text, so that you can see a landscape, for example, through the lettering.

FONTS

You can't use text without using fonts. The most common format is TrueType, which is scalable, meaning it can be used at any size.

We'll show you all the options available when using text, then you can go out and use them in your own projects.

It's tricky, but by creating a path you can add text to it which then bends and follows it to create text on a curve.

VIDEO TUTORIAL

The tutorial at the end of this chapter shows how to create text on a curve.

Text options

Formatting the text before applying it saves on time spent editing and correcting it later

NEW FEATURE
New for PSP 9 is the ability to run text vertically, rather than just horizontally.

Stylish text can make a presentation, cover or poster. There are thousands of fonts available – they just have to be installed into the Windows system to be used in Paint Shop Pro. What's particularly clever about the text system here is that each letter has an out-side and an inside. These can be different colours, and you can also specify the line type that is used to create the exterior border, mean-ing very startling effects can be created with the blandest of fonts. Another advantage of the text being hollow is that you can use a texture, gradient or pattern as the fill content, allowing you to design some very creative typographic effects.

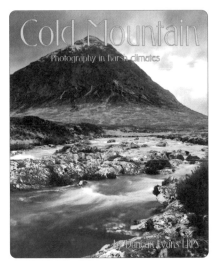

Yellow text with a black border stands out from this monochrome image

---

IN DETAIL TEXT OPTIONS
There's a host of options you can use to tweak your text, here are some of the main ones

1 Each font has a line as its exterior border. The line can be plain or it can be made from any one of a number of fancy designs.

2 This sets how the letters are joined together. The Warp Text box is very important – if it is ticked the text will automatically follow the path it is placed on.

3 The Offset variable specifies how far away from a path the text will appear.

4 Leading is the space between lines. You can adjust it to condense or spread out the text vertically.

5 Kerning is related to leading – it sets the space between characters. If you turn Auto Kern on the program will use the kerning specified for each font. Tracking allows you to alter the overall spacing (not set a specific space) used between the characters by the same amount, regardless of their individual kerning values. It is used when you need to make something fit space of a spe-cific length and, to a certain extent, tweaking this will enable you to do it without cutting the text.

6 The three types of text are Vector, Selection, and Raster. If the raster selection is on the same layer as other raster elements it is merged with them. If it is on its own Raster layer it is easier to deform and alter.

7 The Direction dictates which way the letters and words are arranged on screen. Vertical text is a new feature for PSP 9.

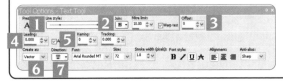

Editing text

In order to use text to your advantage you must first understand how it can be edited

To create text, click on the Text icon in the Tools palette. This turns the cursor into a cross with an A attached to it. Wherever you position this and click is where your text will start. The direction is determined by the Direction drop-down box in the Text palette, which includes the new vertical text. It's a good idea to set the parameters, such as text type, font, size and line style, before you start typing, as it is more work to change these later. The Line Style setting is very important as it not only applies to underlining but the outside skin of the lettering. If you pick a fancy effect it won't just be applied to an underline – be prepared to see your entire text wrapped in it as well.

Create As is a key setting that determines whether the text is vector, raster or selection and creates a layer accordingly, if required. To alter the properties of the text, double-click on it in the Layers palette to bring up the Text Entry box.

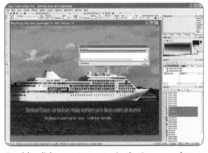

Double-click on a text entry in the Layers palette to bring up the Text Entry box and change the style

ALIGNMENT
The Alignment has no effect when the text only occupies one line. As soon as it goes over two or more, the formatting will be evident.

STROKE WIDTH
Make the Stroke Width bigger but keep an eye on the interior of the text

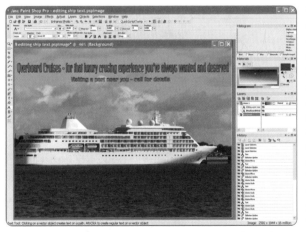

Here the interior colour has been set as transparent and the Stroke Width of both pieces of text has been increased

The Stroke Width is the figure in pixels that defines the thickness of the font's outer skin. If the outer skin and the inside of the font are the same colour, it looks like a one-coloured font. However, it can be advantageous to have a line around text to ensure that it stands out on backgrounds such as pictures. You can increase the Stroke Width to much higher figures in order to create very bold text. Bear in mind that a large increase will reduce the middle colour to a mere streak. Alternatively, if the entire font is enlarged, the interior benefits as the outer skin has a defined size. You can create two-tone text or a number of variations by juggling with the size of the skin and the interior. Don't forget, you can also make the interior of the font transparent, so that the background is visible through it.

LESSON 6
Text on a path 6

Using PSP you can place text on a path of any shape

WHAT WILL YOU LEARN?

■ Resize vector text

■ Blend raster text with images

■ Use patterned stroke lines

■ Paste images into text

While vector text has the advantage of being scalable and flexible, it doesn't offer the great effects that can be used with raster text – like drop shadows or bevel effects. To use these, select the vector text then go to Selections and choose Make Selection From Vector Object. This will create a selection around the text. Press Control+C to copy this to the Clipboard, then go to Edit and select Paste, then Paste As New Layer. Choose a new Raster layer and use the Magic Wand to select each letter in turn. You are then ready to apply any of the standard raster effects.

You can also manipulate and deform text, though how this happens depends on the type you are using. With vector text you can use the Object Selection tool to scale, rotate, shear, distort or apply perspective. If the text is on a Raster layer, either on its own or as part of an image, the Deform tool can be used to change its perspective, scale, shear, or distort. Unlike vector, raster stretches pixels, which can lead to a loss of quality.

NEXT ISSUE

The next issue of *The Official Paint Shop Pro Library* will feature a number of creative projects featuring text – so get practising now!

TIME TO TEXT

STEP BY STEP

1 Load in the picture of Llangollen train station. Click on the text icon and pick a font – we used Estelle Black SF at 48 point. Set it as a Vector with a Sharp Anti-Alias. Put all the other options on default settings. Click on the screen and type in the text. Select Apply then move it around the screen, and position and resize as necessary.

2 Now go to Selections and choose From Vector Object. The text will be highlighted as a selection. Press Control+C to copy this to the Clipboard, then Control+L to Paste as a new layer. Turn off the visibility of the Vector layer and deselect the selection. Click on the new Raster layer, move the text into the right position then use the Magic Wand to click on each letter in turn (holding down the Shift key).

STEP BY STEP

3 Go to Effects/ 3D Effects/ Outer Bevel. Increase the Depth to 58 and select a new colour if required – we've opted for a matt red colour. Check out the various types of bevels but note that unless the text is very large you won't be able to see much difference between them. Click OK and press Control+D to deselect the selection. Go to Layers/ Merge/ Merge All to combine the layers and effectively discard the invisible Vector layer. Hey presto – lovely 3D text on your picture.

4 Now load the picture of Duntulm Castle. Select the Pen tool and click on Draw Point to Point (Bezier Curves). Ensure the Create On Vector box is ticked. Draw a couple of lines with single clicks, using the Bezier Curves function with each click, to bend the lines. When you click, hold down the mouse button and move the handle to bend the line. Ensure the Connect Segments box is ticked so that when you click again it is connected to the previous point.

5 Click the Text icon and select the Sprint SF font at 100 point. The Create As option should be set to Vector. Make the outline colour the same as the fill colour. Ensure the Wrap Text option is ticked. Move the cursor over the curved line until it changes to an A symbol at an angle with a curved line beneath it. Click and enter the text then Apply it. If necessary, move the cursor over the middle so that the Move symbol appears and shift it along the path so that it fits.

6 Go to Selections and choose From Vector Object. This highlights the letters and the inside is the same colour as the outside. Now, switch to the image with the more appealing sky. Mark off a long, thin horizontal section using the rectangular Selection tool and press Control+C to copy. Switch back to the Duntulm image and select the Vector layer. Go to Layers and choose Convert To Raster Layer. Finally, go to Edit and select Paste and Paste Into Selection.

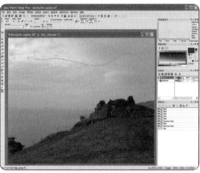

OBJECT LESSON
Besides using the Text and Move tools to select text, you can also use the Object Selection tool if it is on a Vector layer. Simply click, drag and mark the text to be highlighted. The key advantage of this tool is that you can use it to sort multiple objects into order.

VIDEO TUTORIAL #19
 Watch the video tutorial and find out how to create great effects yourself.

ON THE CD

The example images are provided on the CD. Follow the step-by-step guide or just experiment using these images.

CHAPTER 7

Using special effects

Improve your images by adding shadows or using clever lighting, or spice them up with a Displacement Map. Read on to find out more...

When editing photos, many people head straight for the Filter Effects menu and never really leave. The results can be somewhat psychedelic. However, applying filter effects for a specific reason or an artistic purpose is perfectly valid and Paint Shop Pro offers a number of these that you can play around with. PSP supports Photoshop-compatible plug-ins, which is great news because there are thousands of them. When you have a little spare time, take a look at this month's CD as we've provided a collection of 10 freeware plug-in filters for you to use.

PSP's standard effects are accessed via the Effects menu and are categorised thus: 3D Effects, Art Media Effects, Artistic Effects, Distortion Effects, Edge Effects, Geometric Effects, Illumination Effects, Image Effects, Reflections Effects and Texture Effects, followed by any plug-ins loaded and a user-defined option. The Distortion, Edge and Geometric effects can largely be lumped together under an 'image deform' heading. The Art Media, Artistic and Texture effects all march to the same drum and are the most traditional of the effects,

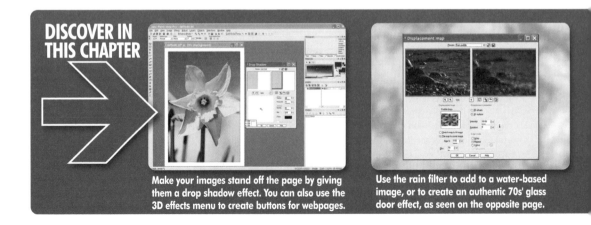

DISCOVER IN THIS CHAPTER

Make your images stand off the page by giving them a drop shadow effect. You can also use the 3D effects menu to create buttons for webpages.

Use the rain filter to add to a water-based image, or to create an authentic 70s' glass door effect, as seen on the opposite page.

seeking to turn the image into another media type. Meanwhile, the 3D category provides specialised Web- or DTP-orientated effects, like buttons, bevelled graphics or drop shadows. These are very useful in their area, as indeed are the Illumination Effects. This is where the Lighting Filter sits, which has lots of potential because it can be used to change the lighting scheme within a picture – this has a particularly dramatic effect in portrait pictures.

To use Photoshop-compatible plug-ins you must first load them into the PSP 9\

Plugins subfolder. Next, go to File and select Preferences/ File Locations. In the File Locations dialog, choose Plug-ins and check that the file location listed is where your plug-ins are stored. Put a tick in the box marked Enable Plugins. This allows PSP to use Photoshop-compatible plug-ins from a variety of sources, considerably expanding the usefulness of this program. The other options here are to limit the plug-in files to the common Photoshop type only, and to allow plug-ins that deal with file formats to pre-filter them without the effect being applied.

GLASS WINDOW

While the Rain filter is intended to give the effect of water splashes, it also bears an uncanny resemblance to that shaped glass effect used in doors in the 70s, as seen above.

Add to the effect you achieve using a natural media brush. The brush strokes filter is best combined with an artistic effect filter.

At the end of the chapter you'll discover how to use the Lights filter to completely change the look of this picture, giving it a film noir aspect.

VIDEO
TUTORIAL #20

Get a basic grounding in setting up plug-in filters and accessing those that are built-in.

Effects Browser

Have a leaf through the various effects on offer, including the filters in the Adjust menu

EXTRA EFFECTS
There's a whole industry in third-party plug-in filter effects. We've got 10 on the CD for you to try

It's been a bit of a trend of late to use a browser for effects so that if you don't like what the current effect is doing you can take a look at all the others. To activate it, go to Effects and select Effects Browser. All the filters from the Adjust menu should be present, as well as those from the Effects menu. The advantage of the Effects Browser is that it presents a thumbnail preview of the type of effect it will apply to your image. Some browsers use a generic image to do this, but the Paint Shop Pro browser uses whatever image happens to be currently loaded in PSP.

A file structure to the left shows all the filters and effects. When you click on one, the right-hand pane shows thumbnails of all the preset options in effect. Click once on a preset, then hit

Apply to use it without modifying the variables. If you click on Modify it switches from the browser to the dialog box of the effect or filter, where you can tweak it as normal.

Use the Effects Browser to preview all the effects and filters in PSP before applying them

CREATING A DROP SHADOW
Drop Shadow is one of the 3D effects

Applying the Drop Shadow effect to a picture with an expanded canvas

Adding a drop shadow effect to something is a neat way of making it stand off the background. Usually this is applied to text, particularly so that it can be seen against a multi-coloured background like a photo. However, it can also be applied to a photo, giving it a subtle finish. To add a Drop Shadow effect to a photo, there obviously needs to be somewhere for the shadow to fall, so the image boundaries need to be changed. First, select the image by pressing Control+A, then go to Image and select Canvas Size. Add 200 pixels, with the image centred, so that you get an extra 100 on every side. Choose white as the new canvas colour. Then, with the extra background and the selection in place, go to Effects/ 3D Effects/ Drop Shadow. Manipulate the direction, strength, amount of blur and opacity of the shadow effect and apply.

Displacement Maps

Don't just warp your image, give it a whole new surface appearance

The Displacement Map effect uses an image pattern (usually greyscale) to distort an image, as though you were looking it through the pattern. It bends and distorts the underlying image and creates a 3D effect.

There are a selection of Displacement Map effects to try out and a handful of variables that allow you to tweak how it will work. The pattern can be repeated, scaled, tiled and made into a 2D or 3D effect. It can be rotated, crystal clear or blurred, and you can set its strength.

The more sensible maps use things like paper types to give the impression that the image was created using it or was painted on it. The wilder designs actively distort and deform the image according to their intrinsic pattern. Whatever pattern you choose, there is certainly a great deal of creative potential here.

Use this Displacement Map to create a puddle effect over the top of the image

BREW YOUR OWN
You can make your own Displacement Maps simply by saving a low resolution JPEG file of a pattern into the PSP/ Displacement Maps folder. The program automatically loads them all.

BRUSH STROKES
Give your photo that Art Media finish you always wanted

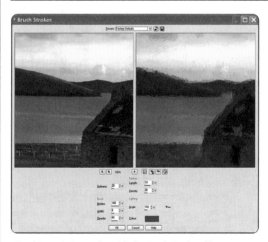

Simulate painting styles with the Brush Strokes filter. It can use variable lighting, brushes and colour

The impact of the Brush Strokes filter effect can vary – it can either turn your photo into a very passable painting or just blur it and apply a few surface-deformation artefacts. The aim of the filter is to render brush strokes on your image and, at their best, these are small strokes that follow the angles and patterns in the photo. This is in fact what makes this filter a real beauty – slapping brush strokes on a regular pattern isn't convincing, but with this filter you can set the angle for the lighting and the strokes themselves follow the angles and paths in the photo. So, horizons can be seen to have horizontal brush strokes while houses have vertical ones.

There are a number of attributes to play with, including softness and the stroke length and density. Even the brush size can be defined, to make it long and thin or thick and bristly, which can give dramatically different results on the same original photo.

Lighting effects

Add a touch of drama to your photos by changing the lighting filters

MATCHING SOURCES

The key factor when adding lighting effects is that they must either match the lighting pattern thrown on the subjects or you must be able to change how the light falls on the subject to match the new light.

While it's not new to Paint Shop Pro 9, the Lights filter is a recent, but very welcome addition to the filter list. When you run the filter (Effect/ Illumination Effects/ Lights) you'll see that there are a few presets to call upon. We recommend you use the factory preset as this uses the lights in a way that is easy to access and manipulate.

The Lights filter can also be edited. The cone of light that determines how wide the arc is can be physically manipulated by dragging the arms on the lighting icon. It can also be done by entering values in the Cone box in the main dialog. This has the advantage that you can give multiple lights the same characteristics. Each lighting icon has a cross with a circle around it – when pulled out the light points sideways across the picture; when pushed back it turns toward the user's viewpoint.

IN DETAIL LIGHTS FILTER

Add dramatic lighting to your pictures with the Lights filter

1 The Preset box contains a list of light positions and colours. Use the default preset to get up and running.

2 The source window shows the original image and the position of the lights. Bear in mind that the actual lighting effect can start from some way off the actual light.

3 These handles control the cone or spread of the light. It can also be set to a specific figure in the Settings box.

4 The preview window shows the light effect in action.

5 The Darkness setting controls how dim the picture outside of the arc will get.

6 Use these icons to select the individual lights.

7 If you don't want to use a light, untick this box.

8 The light can be a neutral grey or you can add a colour gel.

9 Set how brightly the light burns here.

10 The direction can be set by moving the lighting icon or by altering the angle here (10a). The Horizontal and Vertical indicators (10b) allow precise positioning.

11 This sets the smoothness of the lighting effect. Reduce the effect and it becomes coarser.

12 The Asymmetry value determines how balanced the lighting effect is. If it's unbalanced, light will scatter more on one side than the other.

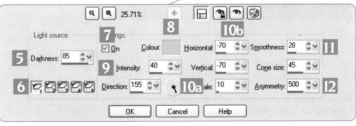

LESSON 7
Use lighting effects

STEP BY STEP

1 We're going to give this picture a moody, film noir feel. Go to Adjust/ Colour Balance, click Channel Mixer and put a tick in the Monochrome box. Set the Red channel to 30%, the Green to 40% and the Blue to 30%. To preserve the original brightness the numbers should add up to 100%. Any less and the picture will be darker, which affects the whites; any more and it will be lighter, risking losing highlight detail.

2 This woman has a net veil, which could be a nightmare to select. So, click the Magic Wand and set a Tolerance of 20. Untick the Contiguous box so that the Magic Wand can pick up all the holes in the net. Click on a white area. This will select virtually all the bits behind the veil, but also the face and chest. Tick the Contiguous box, hold down the Shift key and click on the areas that still need selecting.

3 Swap to the Freehand Selection tool. Hold down the Control key and select inside the figure to remove all pixels that shouldn't be selected. Next, zoom in, hold down the Shift key and select areas of background that should have been selected. Go to Adjust/ Modify/ Feather and set a value of 1. Invert the selection and press Ctrl+C to copy the figure. Go to Paste/ Paste as New Layer.

4 Select the background layer and go to Effects/ Illimunation Effects/ Lights. Select the Factory Defaults preset and click on lights 3, 4 and 5, then untick the On box. This turns them off. Select light 1, and change the Cone size to 27 to make it narrower. Grab hold of the light and move it up so it starts off screen. Repeat the process with light 2. Apply the filter.

VIDEO TUTORIAL #21

Separating the figure from the background is a tricky process, particularly when lighting effects are then applied. Watch how it's done in the video tutorial.

CHAPTER 8

Images for the Web

PSP has a host of tools to make it easy to prepare graphics and construct image maps for use on your webpages

YOU'LL DISCOVER HOW TO...

- Prepare JPEGS
- Optimise GIF transparency
- Create image maps
- Make buttons

As well as the general filters and tools Paint Shop Pro has to offer, there are some Web-specific options, tools and dialogs available.

When producing graphics for webpages you need to keep an eye on the total file size that the user will have to download to view the page. When you are dealing with photographs, file sizes can start to get quite large. The program provides a space-versus-download speed calculator to give you an idea of the demands you are making on the viewer's connection.

JPEG optimisation

All JPEG files are compressed, but you can choose the level of compression to achieve the optimum balance between image quality and file size. PSP also has the ability to save Progressive JPEG images. With these, the user sees a fuzzy version of the full picture, which gradually becomes more detailed as the file is downloaded.

GIF optimisation

GIF files are better used for banners, buttons and illustrations than for photographs, as

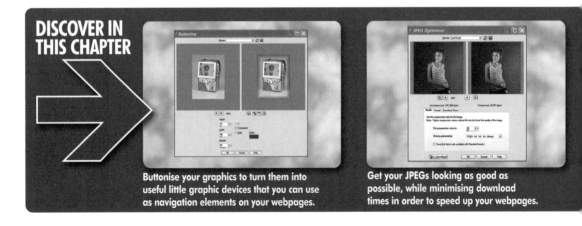

DISCOVER IN THIS CHAPTER

Buttonise your graphics to turn them into useful little graphic devices that you can use as navigation elements on your webpages.

Get your JPEGs looking as good as possible, while minimising download times in order to speed up your webpages.

Material Girl	Fashion
Moody portrait	Dark Angel
Cross process	Street Life
Victorian Whitby	Traditional portrait

they only have 256 colours. You can save the GIF equivalent of a Progressive JPEG, which is called an Interlaced GIF. You can designate one colour of a GIF as transparent, allowing you to create irregularly shaped graphics which 'sit' on top of other graphics.

Creating buttons

A simple dialog box allows you to convert any graphic file into a button. For example, you can create a button using text on a white background, a small picture, or part of a larger picture marked out using the selec-

tion tool. You can then run the JPEG or GIF Optimiser on the button you've produced, to ensure it's as space-efficient as possible.

Image mapping

The Image Mapper allows you to define areas in a picture that act as hotspots for links to other pages on your site, or on the Web. You can also use hotspots to trigger actions and events, which is heading into Web-programming territory. The final tutorial for this chapter takes you through the process of creating an image map, step by step.

CREATING GRAPHICS

You can use the images and buttons that you create in Paint Shop Pro with any website-creation package.

Set the transparency attributes of your GIF banners, and decide how they should look while loading with the interlace option.

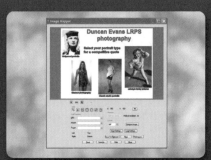

The lesson at the end of the chapter shows how to use a graphic file as an image map complete with hotspots.

Buttonise

It's the easy way to create buttons and objects for your webpages

DOUBLE UP

When creating a button, don't forget to prepare a second version that represents the button being pressed. This will give it a much more professional finish.

Paint Shop Pro has a handy Buttonise filter that allows you to take any graphic object and convert it into rectangular buttons. It can be used in conjunction with the Selection tools, so you can select an area of the image and apply a button effect to it, then make another selection and create a button from that.

You can specify a 'transparent' edge effect for your buttons, but this doesn't make one colour truly transparent – instead, any part of the graphic near the edge is blended with the effect, so it looks like a picture has been pasted over the top of it. Another limitation to be aware of is that the Buttonise filter works in 24-bit colour mode. This means that if you're working with a GIF file (which has only 256 colours), it'll be converted to 24-bit

colour first. It can be resaved as a GIF later, but this involves converting back to 256 colours, which could make the button edge effect look a little coarse.

Here the Buttonise filter has been used to turn each picture into a separate button effect

IN DETAIL USING BUTTONISE
It's quite simple and quick to use

1 The source window shows how your original picture or selection looks without the button effect.

2 Here the button effect has been applied. You can see whether it is infringing on the image contents and if so, adjust it accordingly.

3 The Height and Width are the dimensions of the button effect. Increase these for more chunky-looking buttons.

4 The Opacity sets how smoothly the button effect blends into the edge. Experiment with it for different effects.

5 You'll probably want to leave this on the Transparent option, as the solid one simply gives a thick border effect.

6 It's fine to leave the colour on Black, as it has shades that blend into the colour underneath without affecting it. However, there's nothing to stop you choosing other colours if you want.

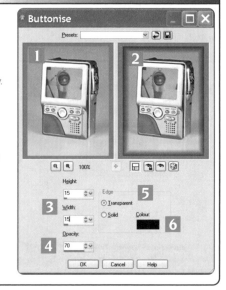

JPEG Optimiser

Compress your images into the optimum format for the Web

SAVE SPACE
The best way to keep file sizes down whilst preserving quality is simply to reduce the image size. A 600x400 pixel picture takes up roughly a quarter of the space that a 1,200x800 image does.

JPEG is commonly the format of choice for photographs, offering 16.7 million colours to GIF's 256. But JPEGs can be large, which is where the JPEG Optimiser comes in.

Go to File/ Export and select JPEG Optimiser. You'll see a three tabs, the first of which deals with Quality. Here you can set the Compression level. Zoom into the effect window to see the level of damage the compression is causing. If a tiny file size is essential, Chroma Subsampling also becomes an option; there are various levels it can be applied at, reducing image size further but causing more degradation.

On the next tab, there's the option to save the file as either a standard picture or a Progressive JPEG (providing viewers with a fuzzy image and adding data as the file is downloaded). If your viewers are likely to have slow Net connections, the Progressive option is the best one to use.

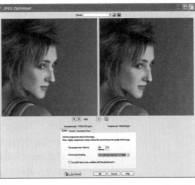

This picture has been heavily compressed. Not only are there square artefacts on the subject, but the background has been affected too

IN DETAIL SQUASH IT
Use the settings carefully to get the right balance between size and quality

1 The source window shows the original image.

2 The results of the compression options will appear here. Zoom in so that you can see them properly.

3 Set the compression here. Any more than 20 will start to degrade the image.

4 Use this option if you really need to save extra space, but beware as it can have a noticeable effect on image quality.

5 If the picture was captured with a digital camera and you want to save the recording details, put a tick in this box.

6 The Format tab allows you to set normal or progressive encoding.

7 The Download tab doesn't provide any options, it just gives you a key to the rough times it takes to download the current file on a variety of connections.

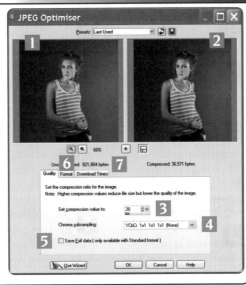

GIF Optimiser

Make the most of your banner graphics with this optimising tool

DON'T GIF IT
Don't save photographs in the GIF format in the belief that they will take less time to download – they won't, and they'll look awful. Use optimised JPEGs instead.

You'll find the GIF Optimiser under File/ Export. On the Transparency tab there are options to use no transparency, use an existing image or layer transparency, or make areas of a specified colour transparent. (Applying a Tolerance value means that colours close to the one selected will also be included).

GIFs don't support partial transparency – something is either transparent or it has a colour value – so the next tab along deals with what to do with images that have partial transparency. You can convert these parts to being fully transparent, use a dithered pattern, or blend the pixels into the background colour.

The Colours tab allows you to specify

how many colours are used. If you reduce this from 256, there's the option to use dithering – where two colours are mixed together with alternating pixels to give the impression of a third colour. You can also opt to use the Web-safe colour palette.

Finally, the Format tab allows you to choose between saving regular files or inter-laced ones (where a crude overall image loads quickly and the detail is gradually filled in).

PC PARAMEDIC

This banner is ideal to use as a GIF image as the white background can be set to be transparent

IN DETAIL GIF OPTIONS
These are the settings you can use to optimise the image

1 This is the original image.

2 Here's the GIF version, showing the effects of all the settings.

3 These are the transparency options, including using none, using the existing transparency, or creating a new area based on a selected colour.

4 The Tolerance sets the amount of variance allowed in selecting coloured pixels for transparency.

5 If your source image has partial transparency, you'll have to tell PSP how to deal with this, because GIFs don't support this feature.

6 If your banner only has four colours, then includ-ing the others in the file format just wastes space. Save space by limiting the colours in the file to the ones you are using.

7 Use the Interlaced option on graphics-heavy sites, or if your viewers are likely to have slow Net connections.

8 The compressed figure shows how much smaller the optimisation is making the image.

LESSON 8
Image mapping

Use hotspots on an image to link to other parts of your website

STEP BY STEP

1 Once you've named the pages you're linking to within your site and have the URLs of external sites, you can use PSP to create the image file that will form the basis of your image map. When it's finished and you've saved it, click File/ Export/ Image Mapper.

2 Increase the size of the window so you can see all or most of the image (use the cross under the image to pan). Select a tool that fits the shape of the hotspot you want to mark – rectangular, circular and freehand shapes are available. In the image window, mark out the area you want the hotspot to occupy. In the URL field, type the address that the hotspot is going to link to.

3 Use the Pan tool (first on left) to resize the hotspot shape, or the Mover (next to Pan) to move the entire hotspot area. In the Alt Text box, enter the text that will appear if the image doesn't. In the target box specify what you want to do with the linked page – setting it to _blank will load the linked page in a new browser window. Finally, use the Format entry to set the format of the completed image mapper.

4 The Rollover Creator lets you set up the hotspots so that they change when the mouse hovers over them. Use something that's the same size as the area being replaced. As each area is completed, the line around them turns red. When you've finished, you can either copy the HTML code to the Clipboard, then paste it into your Web-creation software or save it to the hard drive for later use.

WHAT ARE MAPS?

Image maps contain hotspots that can be defined to link to other webpages when clicked. Any image can be used as the image map source.

CHAPTER 9

Borders, frames and edges

Add a finishing touch to your photographs by paying special attention to the bit most people forget about – the outside

Borders, frames and edges all do different things, but have one thing in common: they are all concerned with adding a finishing touch to the exterior of your image that will either make it more classy, hold in the contents, or give a modern, distressed look.

The border line

A border is basically a canvas extension in a colour you choose. It can be as thin as one pixel, which will give a key line effect around the whole image, or as large as your com-

puter memory and processing speed can cope with. In reality, a chunky border adds weight to the image and holds everything in, particularly if it is darker than the contents. Alternatively, a white frame around a black image lifts it up.

Frame it up

A frame is like the traditional wood or metal object that you put around your pictures and hang on walls, except that it is digitally created and welded onto the exterior of the image. Frames can vary from

DISCOVER IN THIS CHAPTER

Adding a border to your picture is simplicity itself, and provides a smart finishing touch.

Make your digital picture look like it came from a piece of film with this frame effect.

the traditional, to very minimalist and modern, or tacky and vulgar if you like that kind of thing. There are a selection of frames available in Paint Shop Pro, but the list isn't huge and you may want to investigate third-party suppliers if you intend to use a lot of them.

Edge effects

You'll find the Edge effects in the same menu listing as the frames. Edge effects are rather different in that they are designed to eat into and distress the edge of the image. They don't add anything at all, except faded splendour and visual impact.

PSP comes with a small selection of edge effects, but you can also create your own and save them for future use, thereby building up your own portfolio of edge effects. If you're not feeling creative but want more edge effects than PSP offers out of the box, then you can pick up third-party packages like AutoFX's Photo/Graphic Edges 6. This includes over a thousand edges and frames.

MAX EDGES
Use massively destructive edge effects like the one above to give your photos visual impact

Edges nibble into your images, as this spiky little effect shows, but they can give a pleasing faded effect.

There isn't a huge choice of edges available in **PSP**, so why not follow the tutorial and have a go at creating your own?

Borders

Adding a finishing touch to your image is easy with a border effect

CANVAS EXTENSION
This is little more than the expand canvas option, but it's quicker to get to and to use for borders

Possibly the easiest way to make your picture stand out a little more and give it that finishing touch is to add a border, using the Image/ Add Borders option. The border can be measured in terms of pixels or physical size (inches/centimetres/millimetres). The default option is to create a symmetrical addition, and indeed that's what you will need most of the time. Adding a much greater amount to one specific size can be useful though – think of a business card with a picture attachment.

The use of colour should also be carefully considered. It could be complementary for a colour picture, but usually it's best to stick to a black or white border. Black can be heavy if the border is thick, but it will hold the image in place. A white border works best against a dark or black background as it will set it off and subtly lift the image. A thin, two-pixel border can also be surprisingly effective, adding a classy keyline around the image which looks good when printed out.

The five-pixel black border used here frames the image and holds in the light side on the left

BORDER BONANZA
Use the Border option creatively to add your own frame

Loch Leven by Duncan Evans LRPS

Adding a border to this picture only took a couple of minutes, but it's very effective

Of course, there's nothing to stop you from adding multiple border effects to create your own frame, then adding a signature in the space that you've created. This is very straightforward and very effective. Just add a keyline border, then a larger, white one, which forms the gap. Then add a final, thin black keyline border effect again. Add your signature in the middle of that white space, and hey presto – a classy frame.

Frames and edges

Add it to the outside for a frame effect, nibble away at the inside for an edge

To apply a frame or an edge effect, click Image/ Picture Frame – here you'll find all the available effects grouped together. As the frames and edges have shapes and patterns that might not be entirely symmetrical, it can be frustrating to find that a key part of the image is obscured by the frame or edge. Thankfully, you can flip, mirror or rotate the effect. The latter is very useful if, for instance, you have a portrait-orientated picture but want to use a frame designed for landscape-orientation pictures.

Some very subtle and interesting effects can be created if you are using a multi-layered composition, as the edge effects in particular can be applied to the current layer only, revealing whatever happens to be below.

Generally, frames are for the outside of the image, adding to the canvas, and edges are for the inside, eating away at it. However there is the option to use both in the opposite fashion, so the frames compress inside the image or the edge is on the outside.

Here a spiky edge effect has been applied to the image

APPLICATION AREA
When editing edge effects, remember that the grey area is where the picture will be, and the white part is the edge effect.

IN DETAIL EDGES IN ACTION
Check out the options for applying frames and edges

1 This is the frame or edge effect that is to be applied to the image.

2 Some edge effects in particular use an alpha channel to define areas of transparency. These are useful for multi-layered compositions.

3 The preview window gives you a good idea what the effect is going to look like.

4 This option doesn't mean anything unless you are using multiple layers, in which case some very sophisticated framing effects can be created.

5 Frames go round the outside, edges go on the inside. That's the law... though occasionally you might want to break it.

6 If the frame or edge effect doesn't quite work with your image because some important element is obstructed or erased, these options will allow you to move it around.

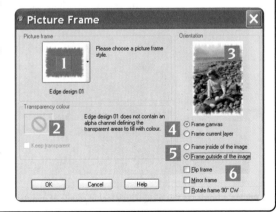

LESSON 9
Custom edges

Can't afford a fancy plug-in, and bored of borders? Create your own edge effect instead

STEP BY STEP

VIDEO TUTORIAL #22
This is a fairly easy exercise and you can produce a number of interesting variations. See how we did it in the video tutorial.

1 Edges eat into a picture, so there needs to be plenty of room around the outside for the damage to be inflicted without it looking cramped. First, create a duplicate layer in the Layers palette and click on the rectangular Selection tool. Mark out a selection inside the edge of the picture to form the boundary of the effect. Go to Selections/ Modify, and Feather the selection by 15 pixels. Then Invert the selection.

2 Select the Paintbrush then choose a brush size that is small enough to fit into the area you have selected. With a picture that is very light, it is advisable to set the foreground colour to black, so that there will be real contrast with the edge effect. Otherwise, set the foreground colour to white. Set the brush Opacity to 50%, unless you want a more wispy effect, in which case set it to 25%.

3 Now sweep across the line of the selection, back and forth as you go around the edge of the image. Go all the way around once, then start again and go back, this time brushing along the very outside edge of the image with a slightly bigger brush. This gives an effect that fades out. Alternatively, concentrate on the inner line of the selection which will give the picture the look of a photo pulled from a scrapbook.

4 Go to Selections and click on Deselect. Change the Opacity of the brush to 15% with a Hardness of 35% for a very feathered edge. Where the edge effect borders the photo, make brush strokes into the main picture area so that it doesn't look like a uniform square with an edge stuck on. Also use this brush to remove parts of the edge effect that don't look quite right. Finally, merge the layers and save.

Part Two
Paint Shop Pro
and beyond

CHAPTER 10

Device integration

Before you can edit your images you'll need to get them onto your computer. We'll tell you how in this chapter

If there's been one advancement in Windows over the years that stands out more than all the rest, it's the diversity of hardware that it now supports and the way it supports it. Paint Shop Pro is able to take advantage of this increased hardware support by interfacing directly with a wide range of connected devices through a variety of means.

The old-fashioned method of connecting the operating system with hardware was to use a TWAIN driver, which described the hardware to the system. The software could then use the driver to access the hardware directly. All PC-compatible scanners used to be TWAIN driven, as did the first generation of digital cameras. Even in the 21st century, some digital cameras still come with a TWAIN driver. To see a list of the TWAIN-compatible hardware installed on your system, from within Paint Shop Pro go to File/ Import/ TWAIN/ Select source. Click on any device in this list, then on Select to set it up ready for acquisition. Now go to File/ Import/ TWAIN/ Acquire to run the software driver pertaining to the hardware. When

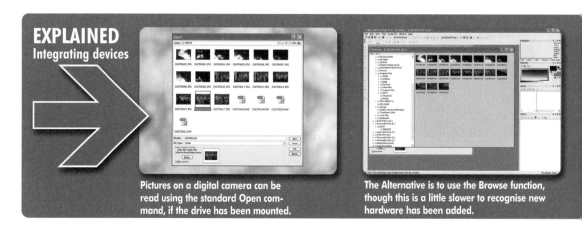

EXPLAINED
Integrating devices

Pictures on a digital camera can be read using the standard Open command, if the drive has been mounted.

The Alternative is to use the Browse function, though this is a little slower to recognise new hardware has been added.

using a scanner, this driver controls all of the hardware's available scanning options. For digital cameras it commonly displays a window with thumbnail previews of the images that are on the camera. Click on any of these then on Download to load the selected images into PSP.

It's now far more common to use fast and stable USB and USB 2.0 cables to connect cameras and scanners to PCs. PSP supports the Windows XP and Me interface protocol known as WIA, which acts in a similar fashion to the TWAIN driver for digital cameras.

However, your camera needs to be WIA compatible for it to work and, unfortunately, most aren't. Instead, when the camera is connected to the computer via USB, it prompts for a driver CD. When installed this assigns the camera a drive letter until it is switched off or disconnected. You can then treat this drive exactly as you would any other on the system – files can be dragged, dropped and copied like files on any drive. As PSP uses the Windows file structure, any drive mounted in this fashion also appears in the Open box and the Browser.

WINDOWS HARDWARE

Although Windows XP can detect and identify any new hardware connected to it, you'll still probably need a software driver to connect to the system.

PSP 9 supports digital camera raw data formats from a number of manufacturers.

The digital camera raw data can be adjusted and for colour casts can be corrected before it even loads into PSP.

Accessing cameras

There are numerous ways of getting your digital camera pictures into PSP 9

TIME SAVER

Possibly the handiest method of getting images on to your PC is to use a card reader. This is mounted as an extra drive and can copy pictures from the memory card, without the camera being present or used.

There are several ways of getting pictures onto your computer or into Paint Shop Pro. If your camera is WIA-compatible, PSP can access the images on it directly via the File/ Import/ From Scanner or Camera menu option. Alternatively you can use a USB connection and the far more common mounted drive system – images can then be viewed using the Open image icon and menu selection (see page 25 for more on opening images). As files viewed using the Open command can be presented as thumbnails, there is little difference between this and the importing method.

Thumbnails can also be viewed using the Browse option (see page 17). This generates the thumbnails much quicker and offers a user-friendly file tree structure. Double-click on a picture icon and it will be loaded directly from the camera into PSP. By dragging and dropping images from the camera or memory card into named folders on your hard drive, you can free up your card without having to process, sort and edit your pictures first.

Use the Browse function to display thumbnails of your pictures. It can also read the EXIF data from the picture, while it is still in the camera

CAMERA WIZARD
Windows can't find your camera? Read on...

When you connect old cameras to Windows using the USB cable, the system sometimes looks at it but decides it can't tell what it is. This is because all new devices, including cameras, report their model and manufacturer to the system, but old hardware doesn't have this feature built-in. The best way of proceeding is to install any software and drivers that came with the camera. If you've mislaid them, Windows has a Scanner and Camera Installation Wizard that allows you to manually select the camera type from a list.

Lost the drivers for your old camera? The Windows Scanner and Camera Installation Wizard may be your only hope

Raw images

PSP 9 is now able to deal with digital camera Raw files

Paint Shop Pro makes a distinction between RAW graphic files and Raw digital camera files. The former are bitmap images with no compression and little header information. Raw camera files are totally different, but are based around the same concept. This is the image from the camera before it is saved as a particular picture format, with or without compression and the relevant header material.

Every camera manufacturer uses a different format for its Raw files. Usually, dedicated software is required to read these, which can be a pain as such software lacks the power or flexibility of PSP. The good news is PSP can read many of the common formats such as those from Nikon, Fuji and Canon. When the file is read in, there is the option to carry out some processing before it is fully opened in PSP and edited using the other tools and filters. When you've finished editing your photo, it can be saved in a regular format such as TIFF.

RAW ADVANTAGE
The Raw format has the quality advantages of TIFFs, but creates files that are 50-75% of the size.

When you connect the camera to the computer via the USB port, Windows XP will present this dialog box

IN DETAIL RAW DATA
Tweaking the Raw picture file is essential

1 This is the Raw picture, showing any enhancements you make using the settings below.

2 These two options are for locking the picture at 100% and scaling it to fit inside the current window size.

3 Use the Mover tool to grab the picture and manoeuvre it.

4 This is the amount of sharpening that will be applied to the file. Be careful when using high settings on landscapes as haloes and artefacts may appear.

5 If you shot the picture sideways on, rotate it to the correct orientation here.

6 Without going into reams of technical detail, if you enter plus values here the picture will be brighter; negative values make it darker.

7 The Auto White Balance can go horribly wrong in indoor shots. Correct it by either specifying the conditions it was shot in or by assigning another white balance setting.

LESSON 10 ![NEW FOR PSP9]
Using Raw pictures

GO FASTER
Raw files can be 12MB in size from a 6Mp camera, so it pays to have a USB 2.0 or a FireWire connection to speed up the image transfer.

STEP BY STEP

1 First, go to File/ Preferences/ File Format Preferences. Select the Raw Camera Data tab and tick both boxes. The top entry means that when the Raw file is opened the Raw File Processing dialog will appear before you load the image. You only need to set these preferences once. Connect the camera to the computer via the USB cable and turn it on. Windows XP will then ask you what you want to do with it.

2 Either choose one of the suggestions or click on Cancel and go to the Browse tool in PSP to navigate through the list on the newly created drive. Double-click on the Raw file you want to load and start the Raw Processing dialog. First you'll need to sort out the picture's orientation – use the Reorientation tools to turn it. Leave the sharpening for now – deal with it from within the main PSP program.

3 When a camera meters a scene, it arrives at an Exposure Value, or EV, ranging from 3 (very dark) to 20 (very bright). Exposure Compensation is the process of manually adjusting the camera to let in, say, a bit more light. It uses the EV scale to do this. The Exposure Compensation value in this dialog allows plus (making it lighter) or minus (darker) to be used in precise increments. This picture needed a value of +0.8.

4 The final setting here contains a list of light sources. If the image has a colour cast, picking the right light source should cancel it out. Alternatively, just leave it set to As Shot if it's OK. Selecting Incandescent has given this picture a very neutral colour, which has potential for tweaking later.

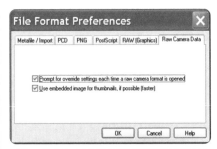

Part Three
The Official Library
Toolkit CD

CHAPTER 11

The Official Paint Shop Pro Library Toolkit

11

If you haven't already upgraded, check out the trial version of PSP 9 before taking a look at the video tutorials, plug-ins and brushes

We are very pleased to bring you a trial version of the updated Paint Shop Pro 9 on the CD. Turn the page for the full instructions regarding its time limit and functionality.

We've also gone filter crazy this month – there are no fewer than 10 plug-in filters provided on the CD. To use them, unzip them to the Plug-ins folder of PSP then go to File/ Preferences/ File Locations. Select Plug-ins in the File types list and tick the Enable option for using external Adobe compatible plug-ins. Tick both folder options, and if you have

saved the plug-ins somewhere else, click on the Add button and add that location to the list. There are eight filters in the TheWorks Series: AlphaWorks, ColourWorks, EdgeWorks, ScreenWorks, EmbossWorks, SwapShop, MasterBlaster, Mezzy. The other two filters are in the Fotomatic series and are Hi-Spot and G-Force.

If you do a lot of brush work, you're in for a treat as you'll find 600 new brushes from Cybia (**www.cybia.co.uk**) on the CD. They range from around 25 to 80 pixels in diameter. Unzip them to the Brushes folder in PSP 9, or

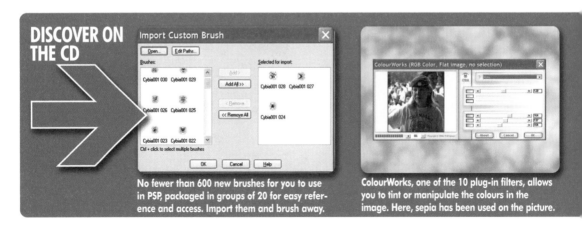

DISCOVER ON THE CD

No fewer than 600 new brushes for you to use in PSP, packaged in groups of 20 for easy reference and access. Import them and brush away.

ColourWorks, one of the 10 plug-in filters, allows you to tint or manipulate the colours in the image. Here, sepia has been used on the picture.

anywhere else you want to keep them. As there are 600, they have been collected together in batches of 20. To load a set go to File/ Import/ Custom Brush, which will open the Import Custom Brush dialog. Click on the Open button and navigate to where they are located. Click on one of the brush files and then OK to bring up the Preview dialog. Either click on Add All to import all the brushes in this file, or select the ones you want and press on Add. Click OK and they will be loaded, ready to use.

And there's more because we also bring

you a demo of the Brush Foundation collection. It allows you to test for compatibility and lets you try out the natural media brushes to see if you like them. This version isn't restricted or limited in any way but it only provides a small selection from the full pack. The full product contains a massive collection of texture brushes for general use. There are 100 different styles with 10 variations in each set, making a total of 1,000 brush tips. If you find the demo useful, you can purchase the full pack from Cybia's Renderosity Store at **http://market. renderosity.com/softgood.ez?Who=cybia**.

ORIGINAL IMAGES
Also on the CD, there are numerous original images from the tutorials and step by steps so that you can follow the processes yourself. Bear in mind that most of these have been reduced in size for copyright reasons and that you are not allowed to use them for any commercial purpose whatsoever. The copyright rests with Duncan Evans at all times.

Give your pictures that spooky medical look using the EdgeWorks filter. It inverts the picture and its tones.

Haven't upgraded to Paint Shop Pro 9 yet? Install the trial version and decide whether you want to buy the upgrade.

VIDEO TUTORIALS
There are 22 video tutorials on the CD showing the interface, tools and tutorials in action. We've also provided original images from many of the tutorials so you can follow the videos yourself.

Paint Shop Pro 9 Trial

Interested in upgrading? Try out the trial version first

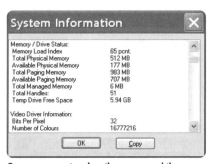

Paint Shop™ Pro® 9

Install:

o Paint Shop™ Pro® 9
o Animation Shop™
o Paint Shop™ Photo Album™ 5 Trial
o Exit

TIME LIMITED
The trial version of PSP 9 is fully functional but is limited to 60 days or 20 uses before it ceases functioning.

Paint Shop Pro 9 is packed with exciting new features. Read on to discover some of them.

The image editor includes some useful filters to remove noise, reduce colour fringing and correct over- and underexposure. Check out our sections on the Digital Camera Noise Removal (page 62), Chromatic Aberration Removal (page 63), Fill Flash (page 66) and Backlighting (page 67) filters to find out how they can improve your shots.

PSP 9 also includes integrated support for Raw camera images from several popular camera models. You can load the Raw image in and, before editing it, set a custom white balance, use exposure compensation and apply sharpening levels.

The other big area of improvement in PSP 9 is the provision of artistic brushes, paint and layers. The Art Media provided include the Oil Brush, Acrylic Brush, Chalk and Pastel, to name but a few. A new Art Media layer allows users to adjust the canvas texture, lighting and wetness properties. There's also a trace function enabling you to create artwork from photographs with ease. Finally, there's a new Mixer palette in which you can blend custom colours together, creating fully textured paint.

TECHNICAL REQUIREMENTS
Make sure your system has what it takes

Minimum System Requirements
Speed: 300MHz processor
Operating system: Windows 98SE, 2000 (SP4), ME, XP
Memory: 256MB RAM
Hard drive space: 500MB free
Display: 16-bit colour with 800x600 resolution
Internet: Microsoft Internet Explorer 6.0+

Recommended System Configuration
Speed: 1GHz processor or faster
Operating system: Microsoft Windows XP
Memory: 512MB RAM
Hard drive space: 500MB free
Display: 32-bit colour display with 1,024x768 resolution
Internet: Microsoft Internet Explorer 6.0+

System Information

Memory / Drive Status:	
Memory Load Index	65 pcnt.
Total Physical Memory	512 MB
Available Physical Memory	177 MB
Total Paging Memory	983 MB
Available Paging Memory	707 MB
Total Managed Memory	6 MB
Total Handles:	51
Temp Drive Free Space	5.94 GB
Video Driver Information:	
Bits Per Pixel	32
Number of Colours	16777216

OK   Copy

Ensure your system has the power and the memory to run PSP 9 effectively

Glossary

The following terms are used commonly in this guide. Other less common terms are explained within the text. Basic terminology can be found on page 10

Artefact: A term for a piece of an image that is not quite right and has been lost because of the file format used. Some file formats, like JPEGs, can reduce file size by compressing the image and losing some of the information, then guessing it back when you load the image. With high compression, this leads to poor quality and the creation of artefacts.

Bounding box: Several tools include rectangles that appear when you use them, like the Vector tools and the Deform tool. The box shows the edges of whatever is selected in the image by the tool. The box normally has eight small rectangles – one at each corner and one at each mid-point. You can grab and drag any to re-size.

CMYK: Cyan, Magenta, Yellow, BlacK. A method of breaking down any complex colour (like a brown) into four primary colours. Professional printers (and some home printers) use this method of colour separation. Paint Shop Pro can use this, but normally uses the more common PC method, RGB (see below).

dpi: dots per inch. The measurement for scanners and printers. A typical printer is 600dpi. Dots are much finer than pixels, so you can set a ppi (see below) within Paint Shop Pro of roughly half your printer's dpi.

EXIF: Exchange Image File. This is an extension to file formats like JPEG that has come about since digital cameras arrived. It includes information about the image itself, such as the time it was taken, camera model, etc. Many people do not realise that their digital camera captures this data.

Greyscale: An image rendered in black, white and shades of grey, rather than colour.

Layer: Paint Shop Pro includes a powerful editing feature called layers. Layers are like onion skins in that you can have one image, or part of an image, on top of another. You can then change how transparent a layer is, so that layers below show through, or perform many special image-editing tasks on layers. There is a Layers palette in Paint Shop Pro that allows you to see and control an image's layers.

Macro: A macro is a form of script that you record through the user interface by asking Paint Shop Pro to record your actions as you do them. Cf Script.

ppi: pixels per inch. Screen measurement used by Paint Shop Pro. See dpi.

Raster: Also known as bitmap. A type of image that consists purely of pixel information. In other words, pixel 1 is this colour, pixel 2 is this colour. The file format has no idea what makes up the image. Photographs are raster images. Raster images cannot be increased in size without loss of quality, because you are creating pixels for which no information existed and the program has to guess them. Cf Vector.

RGB: Red, Green, Blue. A method of breaking down a complex colour into the three primary colours of light (different from the normal primary colours, fact fans). This is the most common way used on PCs. Cf CMYK.

Script: These are text files that contain programming instructions, much in the same way as webpages are constructed. Paint Shop Pro can understand these special instructions and do what the script tells it to, thus automating tasks for you.

Thumbnail: A small rendering of an image, normally shown in Browser view or some Windows views to allow you to see what an image looks like without opening the full-size image.

Tolerance: A value you enter to tell the program how close to a colour you want a pixel in the image to be in order to be classed as being that colour. For example, if you choose a solid yellow, but then make a selection with a tolerance of zero, only that exact yellow will be selected. If you increase the tolerance to 10, then any colours close to that yellow will also be included. Increase it to 20 and colours less yellow will be included and so on.

Tube: Also Picture Tube. A special feature of Paint Shop Pro is Picture Tubes. These are collection of images stored by Paint Shop Pro that you can include in your images by using the Picture Tube tool. They are like flexible clipart.

TWAIN: An old way of connecting scanners and digital cameras to PCs. It worked by allowing the hardware manufacturers to work to one specification, knowing that the software creators (like Jasc Software who created Paint Shop Pro) would write support for that specification in their programs, thus allowing direct access through the File / Import menu.

USB: Universal Serial Bus. Now the most common PC connection technology (most new PCs support version 1.1 and 2, though the interface looks the same). Fast and convenient as you can link hardware together, and connect and remove hardware while the PC is switched on.

Vector: A type of image that is created by mathematics. Lines and shapes can be created and stored as formulae. The advantages are that numbers can be stored in a very small file size and that the shapes they represent are therefore pure in that they can be scaled up in size with no loss of quality. Cf. Raster.

WIA: Windows Image Acquisition. A Microsoft specification that allows Windows and programs like Paint Shop Pro direct access to and control of a digital camera. Designed as a replacement for TWAIN (cf) but most digital cameras will now appear as an actual drive in Windows, bypassing this. See **http://support.microsoft.com/default.aspx?scid=kb;en;293168**.

Next month

THE OFFICIAL PAINT SHOP PRO® LIBRARY

INCLUDES FREE TOOLKIT CD

#07 Creative projects in Paint Shop Pro

An exciting package of creative project ideas, including turning pictures into old prints, producing portraits in the style of David Bailey, and using scripts as quick fixes for your images

Learn how to create fantastic picture projects with this 132-page guide and essential Toolkit CD, helping you make the most of Paint Shop Pro

● Create old fashioned sepia prints with damaged edges
● Produce portraits in the style of fashion-legend David Bailey
● Your name in lights – be the star of a film poster
● How to go monochrome
● Photos into artwork the easy way

Includes Toolkit CD with all-new video tutorials, 10 new plug-in filters, more new brushes and free image-editing utilities

ON SALE IN THE UK 17th FEBRUARY 2005

Index

Pages noted in **bold** are dedicated to the subject. As well as index pages, the video tutorials are also listed, so if you see a VT reference after the page number for a subject, then that number video tutorial is on the CD.

Back Issues

ONLY £8.99 each with FREE P&P (UK only)

ISSUE 1 BEGINNERS' GUIDE
- Get to know the basics of the program and interface
- First steps in image editing
- Understand the digital photography tools
- Improve the colours in your photographs
- Get started with layers, text, Web tools and effects
- CD includes: 34 video tutorials, program updates, full plug-in, 11 free fonts and 10 brushes

ISSUE 2 ADVANCED USERS' GUIDE
- Make better use of the built-in Effects
- Understand painting with Materials for improved photo-editing power
- Learn how to make better selections
- Getting started with Animation Shop
- Discover the power of scripting and start using the built-in scripts
- CD includes: 38 video tutorials, official scripting manual and official tubes, Flaming Pear plug-ins worth US$90, full script editor add-on, two full monitor calibration utilities, 10 new brushes, 10 patterns, 10 fonts and more

ISSUE 3 MASTERING THE TOOLSET
- Every icon in the Toolset e~~~~
- Master the b~~~~ ~~~~ntrol
- Selec~~~~ ~~~~e easy
- Learn ~~~~ adjust images quickly
- Get started with Blend Modes, Brush variances and other power features

SOLD OUT

- CD includes: 41 video tutorials, Buzz simplifier plug-in worth £29.99, full pattern utility, 10 free fonts, 10 brushes, new scripts and more

ISSUE 4 IMPROVE YOUR PHOTOS WITH PAINT SHOP PRO
- Every common photo pr~~~~ solved
- Rescue blu~~~~ ~~~~re
- Re~~~~ssing elements in images
- Restore black and white family prints
- Take your first steps with image manipulation
- CD includes: 45 video tutorials, full commercial plug-in, official Paint Shop Pro picture frames, full digital camera utility, 10 fonts, 15 commercial brushes, 9 brilliant photo scripts and more

SOLD OUT

ISSUE 5 BETTER IMAGE EDITING WITH LAYERS
- Complete introduction to layers
- Learn how to manage layers
- Raster and transform layers
- Blend ranges and use Vector layers
- Improve the performance of PSP
- CD includes Graphicsxtra.com - full commercial plug-in, PSP Thumbnail Enhancement - full program, 10 free fonts, 10 new brushes, plus x-fonter font-management utility